Additional Praise for The Power of WHO!

"Bob Beaudine inspires me! He's my 'Who Coach!' Let him be yours. You will be richer for it."
—Patrick McEnroe, USA Davis Cup Championship Coach, Color analyst ESPN and CBS, USTA GM Player Development

"I believe in *The Power of WHO!* The life lessons and secrets of success Bob Beaudine outlines are invaluable at any point in your career."
—Jerry Colangelo, Chairman Phoenix Suns, Managing Director USA Men's Gold Medal Basketball Team

"The lessons on building and sustaining relationships contained within *The Power of WHO!* can easily be applied to foster success in your professional and personal life. I highly recommend it!"
—Omar Minaya, General Manager, EVP of Baseball Operations, New York Mets

"Bob Beaudine has produced a clear, step by step life plan to harness the power of relationships. Bob is the best in the business today, and in *The Power of WHO!* he shares a lifetime of professional secrets with you. *The Power of WHO!* is a fast read, with powerful insight on every page."
—Steve Bartlett, Former Member of US House of Representatives, Former Mayor of Dallas, Texas, President and CEO of The Financial Services Roundtable

"Bob Beaudine gets you back to the basics with a winning offensive strategy! Start the New Season with *The Power of WHO!*"
—John Calipari, Head Basketball Coach, University of Memphis, Two Time National Coach of the Year, Conference USA Coach of the Year, A-10 Coach of the Year

"*The Power of WHO!* is a stimulating guide of self discovery about leading a happier, healthier and more productive life. This book has opened doors of wonderful memories, long-forgotten, and inspired me to explore avenues of new beginnings yet to come."
—Nell Cahn, Wife, mother of two and National & World Bridge Champion. She is a WBF World Master and ACBL Grand Life Master who resides in Shreveport, La.

"*The Power of WHO!* is about more than just relationships. It is life-changing! It forces you to look inside yourself and it challenges your conventional thinking."
—Rick George, Executive Vice President and COO PGATOUR

"Bob Beaudine has figured out what makes the world turn! *The Power of WHO!* is without question the answer we have been searching for on why and how to be successful. It's a must read!"

—June Jones, Head Football Coach SMU, National Coach of the Year, Former Head Coach-Atlanta Falcons, San Diego Chargers

"*The Power of WHO!* is rich in wisdom and a must buy for those who are searching for their dream job or calling in life. Bob Beaudine is my career coach and through his touching stories, humor and life lessons in this book, he will become yours as well."

—Ian McCaw, Director of Athletics, Baylor University

"Bob's book explores a new way to think about and appreciate what you already have. It is also a wonderful reminder that we should respect all the relationships we are fortunate enough to create in our journey through life."

—Gregg Tryhus, Entrepreneur, President/Owner of Grayhawk Development Inc.

"You can read *The Power of WHO!* in one day but the message will last you a lifetime!"

—Steve Orsini, Director of Athletics, Southern Methodist University

"When you discover that You Got '*Who*,' then . . . No one and I mean No one, comes into our house and pushes us around!"

—Daniel "RUDY" Ruettiger, internationally acclaimed author, speaker, student athlete—University of Notre Dame

"For nearly three decades, Bob Beaudine has enlightened the industry leaders in sports with his wise counsel, thoughtful insights and entertaining illustrations to identify the best and brightest talent available for each specific challenge and to grow our business. Now, he is using that same knowledge and expertise to help you develop your 'who' and capture the job of your dreams."

—David Baker, Former Commissioner of the Arena Football League, Former Mayor of Irvine, California

"*The Power of WHO!* is a Must Read for anyone who desires to have their Dreams Become Reality. It will make you laugh, cry, think, and most of all inspire and inform you on how to reach all your Goals and Dreams. Thank you Bob Beaudine for sharing this with us!"

—Scott Drew, Head Basketball Coach, Baylor University

"Two times in my life so far, Bob Beaudine has been my 'who.' The first encounter was to the benefit of my oldest son and his dream job. The second occasion literally extended the life of my dad's best friend. So, I have experienced first hand 'The Power of WHO!' from the author himself. Bob has not only written a very powerful and practical book, he walks the talk."

—Randy Frazee, author, *Making Room for Life*

THE POWER OF WHO!

YOU ALREADY KNOW EVERYONE
YOU NEED TO KNOW

BOB BEAUDINE
WITH TOM DOOLEY

CENTER
STREET®

NEW YORK BOSTON NASHVILLE

Center Street
Hachette Book Group
1290 Avenue of the Americas,
New York, NY 10104
www.centerstreet.com

Center Street is a division of Hachette Book Group, Inc.
The Center Street name and logo are trademarks of
Hachette Book Group, Inc.

Printed in the United States of America

First Edition: January 2009

20 19 18

The Hachette Speakers Bureau provides a wide range of authors for speaking events. To find out more, go to www.hachettespeakersbureau .com or call (866) 376-6591.

The publisher is not responsible for websites (or their content) that are not owned by the publisher.

Library of Congress Cataloging-in-Publication Data
Beaudine, Bob.
    The power of who! : you already know everyone you need to know /
Bob Beaudine.—1st ed.
        p. cm.
    Summary: "This book shows that you already know everyone you need to know to get anything you need in life"—Provided by the publisher.
    ISBN-13: 978-1-59995-153-9
1. Success—Psychological aspects.   2. Social networks.   I. Title.
BF637.S8B377   2009
158—dc22

2008027725

To the love of my life, a true gift of God, my wife Cheryl. Her encouragement, patience, and late nights listening to and advising me on all the changes made each day has allowed this book to reach your hands. But best of all, thanks for "believing in me!" That of course . . . changes everything. I love you!!

To my three amazing and talented daughters Aly, Jenny, and Rachel, who inspire me to be a better man, father, and friend. Thank you for reminding me daily that I Got "Who"! I am so proud of each of you!

To the memory of my Dad and Mom (Frank and Martha Beaudine) whose core values, wisdom, and love fill the pages of this book. My Dad was my best friend, mentor, and partner in business for twenty years! He made coming to work a joy! My Mom was the best example of unconditional love I have even known. I miss you both!

CONTENTS

ACKNOWLEDGMENTS

Writing a book to encourage and inspire people about how to go for their dreams and goals has been a dream of mine for many years. I finally reached a time in my life when I gave myself permission to stop dreaming and start doing. In the process I learned the truth that we're all created "A Cup Short" of greatness. Because in order to accomplish the formidable task of authoring this book I had to remember, reach-out, and re-connect with my *"Who."* I had to seek out and find my real diamonds, those special friends who love me and wanted to help in any way they could just for the sheer joy of seeing me successfully complete this book. I've learned firsthand it really is all about the Power of *"WHO!"*

So many people need to be thanked for their encouragement and assistance while writing this book. Jay Johnson was there at the very beginning as my first editor and was a great help and encouragement to me. Big thanks to Tom Dooley who has to be singled-out and acknowledged for all his time, creativity, and wonderful literary skills. One of my most enduring and trusted friends, Mark Kane read through an early manuscript, saw great potential and helped tremendously with the organizational structure of the book. Hugs and thanks to my incredible sister Nancy Berg, who has always been a clarifying sounding board in my life as well as with this book. To my talented niece Lisa Apple, thank you for all your support and to my right hand assistant/clone Katy Young who listened to and read all the drafts as they came off the printer—Thank you, Katy!

Thanks to my agent Jan Miller—you're simply "The Best!" A Big thank you to both Jan and Nena Medonia for your friendship, confidence in me, and your passionate belief in the Power of *"WHO!"*

To Harry Helm and the superb creative team at Hachette/Center Street. Thank you, Harry! You've been a catalyst behind making this book into something extraordinary.

So many of my *"Who"* friends read the manuscript, offered valuable input, gave timely encouragement and patiently listened to me as I talked endlessly about the Power of *"WHO!"* I know I don't have to mention their names but I want to: Jordan Bazant, Dr. Jim Beckett, Robin Blakeley, Amber Brown, Carlyn Davis, Ray Davis, Keenan Delaney, Homer Drew, Scott Drew, Todd Duncan, Jim Fiore, Fran Fraschilla, Ernie Frausto, Randy Frazee, Joe Galindo, Mike Golub, Kathleen Hessert, Stewart Hunter, Blake Judkins, Alyse Kobin, Ian McCaw, Jim McMahan, Ed Perrin, Mike Reilly, Dave Savage, Dave Scullin, Melissa Segura, Terdema Ussery, Doyle and Marjorie Whitaker, and Debbie Yow.

Finally, there is one more very important individual I want to thank. You! Thanks for holding this book in your hands. May the message of "Doing life with your Friends" transform your thinking into a whole new realm of "Living Large!" I'd love to hear from you and how the Power of *"WHO!"* has impacted your life. Go to: www.powerofwho.com and tell me your story.

INTRODUCTION

A friend is someone who knows the song in
your heart and can sing it back to you when
you have forgotten . . . the words.

—AUTHOR UNKNOWN

What if each of us had been given key relationships in our lives that have been specifically placed there to help us in ways we never imagined? And what if those special people were not just happenstance acquaintances but were, instead, strategic relationships meant to be actively involved in helping us find that place in life we always dreamed about? Could it be that we've missed the simplicity behind this mysterious thing called *destiny?* What if the real problem of finding your dream or achieving that goal isn't about who you don't know, but whom you've neglected?

As CEO of Eastman & Beaudine, the nation's leading executive search firm in sports/entertainment (and other very cool, high-paying jobs), I've spent over twenty-five years placing superstar executives in some of the highest positions in the country—running major league teams, cruise lines, studios, networks, Olympic bodies, and major college athletic programs, just to name a few. These individuals have become masters in their chosen fields of endeavor, qualifying them to maximize the use of their unique gifts and talents. In some cases they received diplomas from institutions of higher learning that specialized in their fields. However, in many instances, their formal education had little to do with their success. In each case, they joyfully and willingly submitted themselves to a particular discipline simply because they were drawn to it by some pre-wired, internal radar that acted upon them like a homing signal. Following that signal led them to a place where they are now enjoying the rewards and satisfaction that accompany these top positions. How did they get there? What's their secret? Did they post a "Dear Sir" letter and résumé on Monster.com? I don't think so! No, instead, they discovered the unique but almost universally overlooked strategy that I am going to outline for you in the pages that follow.

My purpose in writing this book is to introduce you to the "100/40 Strategy." This revolutionary concept will get you moving toward your dreams and goals in ways you never imagined possible. It's like finding a treasure map that's been hidden away just waiting to be discovered. Surprisingly, the "100/40 Strategy" is not some new experimental theory. Our firm has time tested this unique approach for over forty years and seen it work successfully time and time again. Throughout this book I'm going to challenge many widely held, preconceived notions. One of which is the popular concept of networking.

> **[!]** Take everything you have ever heard or learned about networking and just throw it out. That's right. Throw it out . . . as in jettison, dump, expel, cast out, in other words . . . fuh-ged-aboud-it!

I can make such a radical statement because, based on my twenty-five-plus years in the executive recruiting business, I can tell you unequivocally:

{!} Networking as we know it is crap.
It doesn't work!

However, the strategy I'm going to reveal to you *does* work. I know it works because for most of my adult life I've been intricately involved at the highest executive levels, not only implementing it myself, but also watching others use it with great success. Like most truly great things in life, it's simple. So simple, in fact, that most people just don't see it. It's like that "hidden" bridge that Indiana Jones had to cross in order to save his father. The bridge was there, but he just couldn't see it until he stepped out onto it.

I'm going to show you this "hidden" bridge and lead you across. Then I'm going to take you to the map that reveals the rest of the pathway to your hidden treasure. You're going to discover what it means to connect with what I call your *"Who."* Along the way your passion is going to be reignited, and you'll, once again, believe that what you've only dreamed about is actually possible.

WHATEVER I'M DOING, IT'S NOT WORKING!

Sixty-nine percent of the country believes that a bad day at the beach is better than a good day at work.

—GALLUP POLL

Just as we aren't born with all the skills we need, neither are we born with a strategy for living. We learn about life by living it, by pushing out on life while life pushes back on us. This is how we create our own space. Old sayings are still around because they usually contain an element of truth. "Life begins at forty" is one we've all heard. It's true because the first twenty years of your life is programmed and controlled by others. The next twenty years is often spent working out a lot of the stuff that was put in during the first twenty. Somewhere around forty you begin to take ownership of your life. It's here that youthful dreams begin to reawaken. It's also here where you discover that some of your old strategies for living are going to need realignment if you're to successfully pursue your dreams and goals.

All our lives we've been told that if we work hard, keep our head down, and mind our p's and q's, everything will eventually work out. Really? If that were true, then what happened to the dream? What I hear more often in my role as an executive recruiter is something like "I'm no closer to my dream than I was yesterday. If anything, it feels even further away. I feel stuck—stuck in a rut."

But there's the paradox. My life is filled with so many good things already. I'm blessed. Sometimes I may even feel a little guilty about wanting something more. But that's actually part of the problem. The things I'm blessed with are the very things that crowd out the dream. My life is filled to overflowing. I'm like an aircraft carrier with so much stuff on the deck there's no room left for anything else to land. I know the dream is still out there, but it's become a little fuzzy. It's just not as clear. A lot of this stuff on my deck needs to be moved somewhere else or just tossed overboard. I sometimes find myself wondering, "Can I even get there from here anymore? Can I make enough money in my current job, which I don't particularly like, so that I can start doing what I always wanted to do?" The short answer is "Probably not."

Here's more bad news. Only a small percentage of people actually end up living their dream. You may have asked yourself on more than one occasion, "Why that person and not me?" I've heard that question asked many times over many years in countless interviews. Surprisingly, I've discovered that individuals who are willing to make even a few slight course corrections were able to alter the entire trajectory of their lives. At first a lot of these people thought they needed an extreme makeover, but the good news is that just a small change in strategy makes all the difference.

Out of Sight, Out of Mind

*Inside each and every one of us is one true authentic swing,
something we was born with. Something that's ours and ours
alone. Something that can't be taught to you or learned.
Something that's got to be remembered.*

—STEVEN PRESSFIELD, *THE LEGEND OF BAGGER VANCE*

Hidden somewhere between laws and principles are universal powers that most people not only ignore but are unaware even exist. These silent powers have tremendous influence in our lives every day. For example, love is neither a law nor a principle but no one would deny its force and impact on our lives. The "Power of Love" is so dominant it's felt and experienced by all people everywhere. Another universal power is Darkness. It renders us unable to see. The only way to overcome the "Power of Darkness" is with light. Interestingly, light can be measured but not darkness.

But there is yet another unseen power that works with equal or even greater force than love or darkness. It operates below the surface of our conscious awareness but with such profound force that it must be considered one of the supreme concealments of all time. This force is the "Power of Forgetfulness." It can secretly overtake our thoughts and emotions like a giant glacier silently advancing through a canyon. The "Power of Forgetfulness" can be all-encompassing as in people with Alzheimer's disease or other kinds of dementia. Or, it can be as benign as not remembering where you left your keys. In its more subtle and dangerous forms, however, it can undermine your dreams and professional life in often devastating ways.

Imagine you're in a science fiction movie. You're on a university campus walking down a large hall on your way to class. But your schedule is so overloaded you've become confused and disoriented. You can't remember where your next class is or even your professor's name. Suddenly you hear a strange noise coming from behind. You turn to see a huge, black blob rolling toward you overtaking everything in its path. The "Power of Forgetfulness" operates in much the same way. In the midst of our full schedules and demanding priorities it rolls into our minds causing us to forget the truly important things in life. A divorce, loss of a job, death of a loved one, and other crises only serve to increase the "Power of Forgetfulness."

For example, the person who just got laid off after fifteen years is experiencing some level of trauma. The degree of this anxiety is exacerbated by the fact that this person just read in today's newspaper that six thousand other people in the same field also just lost their jobs. Now they're all going to be out there looking for new employment. The feeling of being threatened is as old as the caveman with his fight-or-flight reactions. Only today, instead of our running from or putting a spear into a saber-toothed tiger, our eyes start darting back and forth as our thoughts become flashing questions exploding in our mind's eye like a Fourth of July fireworks display, "What am I going to do now?" "Will I be able to find another job?" "What are people going to think about me?" These are fear questions that tend to paralyze. They all lead to the same emotional place: isolation and fear. But hold it! Wait a minute! The truth is you're not alone, you're not isolated.

When we're feeling threatened it can become very difficult to tell ourselves the truth. The fog rolls in and takes up residence in our minds and we're not able to think clearly. Hence the expression "I've been in a fog." It's like you need a red light on the dashboard of your brain that starts flashing whenever you get fearful, fretful, or forgetful. This blinking red light is an "anti-blob" device that sends you an instant message that says, "You are about to be overtaken by the 'Power of Forgetfulness.' You're in danger of losing yourself. Stop immediately and call a 'Who' friend."

What is a *"Who"* friend?

■ A *"Who"* friend will call a halt to fearful thinking by insisting you stop listening to your own negative self-talk. In the face of those lies they will start speaking truth, the truth about your value and uniqueness, the truth about your accomplishments, and the truth about the value of your dreams and goals.

■ A *"Who"* friend will intercept you on the dark path you've taken and redirect your steps back on to the path of light. They know you, care for you, and will remind you that you have a future and a hope.

■ A *"Who"* friend knows your true identity and won't let you forget it. When the "Power of Forgetfulness" tries to roll in like a blob—you need your *"Who."*

Many of us have gotten sidetracked and forgotten our original dream, spending our lives doing derivative work. This memory lapse has become epidemic. We have less and less time to calmly think about the direction our lives have taken and reflect on our current course.

Like those black holes out in space that suck in everything around them, the obligations and busyness of our everyday lives can drain our energy and take up all our time. In the process, our true desires can get diminished and we begin to forget. The "Power of Forgetfulness" has affected too many otherwise successful people. When you forget your "True Authentic Swing," you can be drawn, inexorably, into an apathetic attitude that breeds cynicism—the tool of the lazy thinker.

Lucy tells the hapless Charlie Brown:

"You know, Charlie, life is like a deck chair. Some people place their deck chair so they can see where they're going. Some turn it around to see where they've been. Others, Charlie, place their deck chair right in the middle of the action to see what's going on all around them." Charlie sighs and says, "I'm just trying to get mine unfolded!"
—CHARLES M. SCHULZ

Some of us are a lot like Charlie. We're so busy just dealing with job and life issues that we can forget some of the important things so essential to who we truly are. You've probably had the experience of checking your pockets, looking around because you sense you've forgotten something. But you just can't think of what it could be. Perhaps it's a distant dream that's still alive, so the sensation keeps popping up, but it's been so long since you've consciously thought about it that you no longer connect the sensation to the dream. Is it possible that you once dreamed of living a different life from the one you're living now but just can't remember—something for which you're uniquely and wonderfully "wired"? As an executive recruiter who has talked with literally thousands of job seekers over the years, I can tell you there are many, many individuals who are seeking something *else* but missing something *more*.

A LESSON IN DESTINY

Perhaps there has been a time in your life when you felt you shouldn't try to accomplish what you always wanted to do because it looked like the odds of succeeding were against you. Don't be discouraged when a door is closed. It's simply a message telling you that this isn't the right one for you. Stay alert. There's another one opening that will lead you to something better.

I met George W. in 1983 while planning a political event for his dad (then vice president) and President Ronald Reagan. We couldn't get either of the two fathers to come speak at our event, so we did the next best thing—we invited their kids: George W. and Maureen Reagan. When my wife, Cheryl, and I picked up George W. at Love Field in Dallas, I expected to see Secret Service and an entourage of helper bees swarming the vice president's son. But to my surprise, there was no one with him. The future president of the United States came off that Southwest Airlines flight from Midland, Texas, wearing the basic uniform of a Texas oilman: a blue work shirt and jeans. He even carried a backpack. George W. was down to earth and charismatic and had an engaging smile. It wasn't long before he made Cheryl and me feel like we were his closest friends, partly by his endearing style of calling me Bobby instead of Bob. Nobody had called me a nickname since college. Through the years, this term of affection went from Bobby to Bobby Boy. We hosted George throughout the event. Watching him, my wife and I both commented that he seemed naturally gifted with the skills needed for this type of political fund-raising event. He made friends easily and seemed like he cared about those he met. He also had one exceptional skill that cannot be learned. When he first meets you, he has the rare ability to create a special moment just between the two of you. He would put a hand on your shoulder or tell a story or a joke as if it were meant just for you. Had I been more perceptive perhaps I would have recognized some of the clues that indicated greater things to come in George W.'s future.

Over the next three to four years I would run into him at the airport as we were both headed to New York on business. He would always say, "Let's sit together," and he would share what was going on in his oil business and later the beginnings of his role in his dad's campaign for the presidency. George W. had been asked to join his dad's inside tactical team, and he was very passionate about that role. When he talked about it you could sense his energy rising. At that same time I was slowly moving my search practice toward sports. Since sports was one of his passions, he loved hearing about the types of assignments I was handling for the NBA, PGA Tour, USTA, or Major League Baseball. We would share cabs to our respective meetings or hotels and then go our separate ways.

Within three years George W. became managing partner of the Texas Rangers. He loved America's greatest pastime. He was the one who recruited Nolan Ryan to pitch for the Rangers, which, to George W., was like getting Billy Graham to join your local church. After several years as owner of the Texas Rangers, he started being encouraged to make a run for governor of Texas. Simultaneously, the announcement hit the papers that I had been selected to handle the search for the commissioner of baseball. Next day, I received a phone call from George W. giving me a hearty "Congratulations, Bobby Boy!" He invited me to come over to his office at The Ballpark at Arlington to talk about the search.

Following a long discussion about the game of baseball, he turned the conversation in a different, more serious direction. He told me he was in a tough predicament and had to make a decision quickly. The decision to be made was whether to begin a run for governor against the very popular incumbent, Ann Richards, or try to land the job as commissioner of baseball. "Bobby boy," he said, "You might as well get me the commissioner's job because I don't think I can beat Ann Richards."

Amazing, huh? The man who would become president of the United States for two terms almost made the wrong choice. He was seeking something else but missing something more. After some very detailed research I came back to George W. to report that the timing seemed to be wrong to pursue the job as commissioner. About that same time Karl Rove, his closest aide, had been doing his own research and concluded that the timing was right for a run for the governor's office.

What if you and I could slip inside a time machine and go

back to my meeting with George W. What if when he said that he didn't think he could win the governorship, we said, "Whoa! George, we've seen the future and you're going to win the governorship not once but twice. Then you're going to run for president and win that twice!" He probably would have said, "You guys are crazy. I can't beat Ann, let alone win the presidency. Have you forgotten I'm the son of a president? You know the odds of my winning? Besides, I have a past." Then we would say, "Yes, but none of that matters because you're destined to become president."

It's interesting to look back and see how the patterns woven into the fabric of our circumstances have led us to where we are now. Listen, if the guy who became president almost missed the clues to his destiny, it's easy to see how we could make the same mistake. The point of this story is: if you're going to fulfill your destiny in life you're going to need some wise friends and advisers to help you see a vision of your future that, perhaps, you can't see yourself.

SETTING A COURSE AND STICKING TO IT

One of the big lies many of us tell ourselves is that our current position in life disqualifies us from achieving our dreams and goals. Some of the common phrases I've heard are "It's too late for me. I'm too old," or "I'm too young," or "I'm too . . . whatever." Is that true? No! It's absolutely not true. You're never too early or too late in life to begin walking on the pathway of your dream. One thing is absolutely certain: the future is on the way. Ready or not, here it comes.

The only really important question you need to answer is

{!} What am I doing right now to steer my life in the direction of the future I truly desire?

In sailing, when you set a course for a destination, it's necessary to stay on that course until you arrive. Bad weather (unforeseen circumstances) might blow you off course temporarily but, as soon as possible, you reestablish the correct heading. The same is true of your destiny. Set the course of your desired future and stick to it. Many don't. They start out with the best of intentions but when the "winds of life" blow them off course they just go with the flow and never get back on track. Because of "forgetfulness," you can lose your ability to watch carefully, and so end up just taking life as it comes . . . or worse, crashing on the rocks.

Discernment is the ability to see things deeply—beyond the obvious and below the surface. A hawk soars along hunting for prey hiding in the brush. Because of its extraordinary eyesight the hawk sees what's hidden just under the ground clutter and so gets it's reward. Much of life is camouflaged. Discernment is like having the eyes of a hawk. It enables you to see below the surface of things. If you're going to successfully traverse the unpredictable, often rough and treacherous waters of life you'll need the ability to read the currents below.

You're heading somewhere right now. Life is in motion. Do you like your current direction? Who's steering the ship of your life? Do you have a firm grip on the wheel or have you been on autopilot for so long you forgot where you were supposed to be going?

It's way too depressing and frustrating to have dreams, goals, and a vision for where you want to go but no way to get there—or even an inkling of how to get started.

Take hold of the wheel, you're closer than you think . . .

THE DISCOVERY

Something profound was going on beneath the surface, something that I would later come to understand as a dynamic principle at work. I began to notice it operating in the lives of people with whom I would interact. But it took me a while to connect the dots on exactly what it was. I soon discovered that this principle has always been there but because of its subtle nature tends to remain hidden. It's like gravity and wind—you can't actually see them, but their effect is obvious. This powerful principle has been utilized by successful dream seekers throughout time. It's not complicated; it's really very simple. Here it is:

> **You already know everyone you need to know.**

Before you balk at the simplicity of that statement, let it sink in a bit. I'm telling you it's true. I've seen it work over and over again. Let me say it again. *You already know everyone you need to know.* Please go back and read it once more, and this time read it aloud. You might say to yourself, "Okay, fine. Got it, next." Or you might completely dismiss it as not important and totally miss out on how this principle can work for you. Don't make the mistake of thinking you don't already know enough people who can help you on your quest. It's really not the best use of your time and energy to start sending e-mails out to people you don't know or having lunches with strangers. I have great news for you. You Got *"Who"!* I promise you do.

If you really want to pursue a worthy goal or make a significant change in your life, you don't go external in your approach, you go internal. Here's what most people do: they start looking outside their *"Who"* network thinking their success will be found "out there" somewhere. It's a false notion to think that your success will come from a bunch of people you don't know. This may be like a little cold water in your face, but if your being naive with unreal expectations of others it will save you some disappointment. Don't expect strangers or even acquaintances to care about you or your goals unless they perceive a desired benefit for themselves. That may come across as a little harsh or abrasive but it's really not. I don't mean to infer that people are going to be unkind just because they don't know you. Not at all. Most people will treat you with civility and courtesy. I do mean that the caring quotient goes way up as a relationship deepens. So cultivate your "field of dreams" with your *"Who"* friends.

> **{!}** You already know someone right now who knows the person who will help you achieve your goal or hire you or introduce you to the person you need to meet.

What do you believe you could accomplish that looks way too outlandish to achieve, but deep down inside you know if you got the shot you could do it? I'm not talking about a promotion here. I'm talking about a seismic shift that would change the entire trajectory of your life. Is it writing a book, learning to fly, losing thirty pounds and getting into shape? Is it starting your own company, devoting your full energies to your passion? It could be in sports, music, the arts, charity, or politics. What's hindered you from getting off the dime? I'll tell you. You haven't employed the "Power of Partnering." If you're going to write a book, you'll need a good editor and someone to read it to who will be a sounding board. If you're serious about becoming a pilot you'll need a flight instructor. And if you're going on a diet and getting in shape you'll need a program and a good trainer. Now don't miss the obvious here. Each one of these endeavors and a thousand more you could name require a certain level of personal involvement with others. People serve as *catalysts*. By definition, a *catalyst* is an agent that speeds up a process, sometimes exponentially. Other people provide the power to help you achieve your goals a whole lot quicker than you could ever do it on your own.

THERE IS DIFFICULTY AT THE BEGINNING

Beginning is the key to everything! What do you need? Maybe it's something as simple as an introduction, or perhaps a loan, or just someone who will listen and offer some good advice and encouragement. Maybe you feel you lack the courage or self-confidence to start doing what you've always dreamed of doing. But you'll be amazed at the sense of empowerment you feel as you take those first steps. Things will start to fall into place. Life will begin to make sense again. Trust me; I do this for a living.

If I challenged you to stop right now and refocus your efforts on pursuing a lifelong dream or even a short-term goal, what would it be? Once you answer that question I have two more. Who would you call for assistance and how many would you call? Have you ever stopped long enough to think about your *"Who"* network? You might say, "I don't have a *'Who'* network!" I'm telling you, you do! You Got *"Who"*!

Knowing "WHO" to Ask

Adversity seems to be woven into the very fabric of life. It seems to come out of nowhere and, of course, always happens at the worst possible time. The important question is if the bottom dropped out for you, who would you turn to for help?

In the classic movie *It's a Wonderful Life*, Jimmy Stewart plays the part of George Bailey who lives in the small town of Bedford Falls. He dreams of seeing the world, so he works in the family business to save enough money to leave town. But at the very moment he's about to realize his dream, adversity strikes. His father dies. George is pressed into service taking care of his dad's old savings and loan in order to keep it out of the hands of their unscrupulous competitor, the evil Mr. Potter.

His life turns in exactly the direction he had tried to avoid. Can you relate? Has there been some adversity in your life? Have you had some hopes and dreams stymied?

George doesn't leave that day to see the world; he stays in Bedford Falls and builds a truly wonderful life. He develops and cherishes his friends, loves his beautiful wife and family, and successfully rebuilds the town. And he does it all with passion! But then adversity strikes again. George entrusts a large bank deposit to his uncle Billy. His uncle misplaces the deposit and the money is stolen. Eventually, it ends up in the hands of the evil Mr. Potter, who hides it. When George hears about the loss, he panics. Facing bankruptcy and possible jail time for fraud, George immediately does what you or I would do. He goes to those who know him, who love and trust him. He turns to his friends, right? Wrong! Unaware who has stolen the money he goes to Mr. Potter for help! Isn't it interesting that George seeks help from the one man guaranteed not to provide it? We do that, don't we? Pride often prevents us from asking for help from those closest to us. Why? Because we're embarrassed or even humiliated and don't want our friends to know what's happened. The foolishness of pride is that it pretends to be self-reliant. Pride is the Great Pretender. The truth is friends need each other. How is it we enjoy helping our friends but won't let them enjoy helping us? So we'll pull a "George Bailey" and resort to looking to people who don't know us or give a rip about us. Big Mistake!

Even after Mr. Potter sends him away empty-handed, does George wise up and go to his friends? No. George becomes so depressed he considers jumping off the nearest bridge. How is that possible? When you look back on some of your toughest times, you understand what George is experiencing. His back is against the wall. He's in a blind panic, paralyzed with fear, not able to focus on anything but the problem. It's as big as Mt. Everest with seemingly no way out. Where do you turn? "Who you gonna call?" Maybe you recently lost your job or you're looking at a mountain of debt. Perhaps you lost someone dear to you. If so, then you know how George is feeling. Helpless, defeated, and full of anxiety. We have a word for that. It's called *hopelessness*.

Luckily for George, his wife, Mary, has already begun to reach out to his friends all over the city and beyond. They immediately come to help their friend in his time of need. That day George rediscovers one of life's greatest and most valuable secrets—the Power of *"WHO!"*

Everyone has a *"Who"* network, a "community of friends" that's been built up over many years with love and unconditional giving. These are friends who genuinely care about you and share your core values. This particular network of friends, if asked, will actually come to your aid. They want you to succeed. They want you to achieve your goals. And they love you just the way you are.

Is it possible that all these years you've been sowing seeds with the wrong crowd? Is it possible that someone you already know, someone who likes you, can actually help you? George Bailey would say—YES! Absolutely!

THE KID WHO KNEW HE'D BE A MILLIONAIRE

I met Mark Kane on my first day of college on the steps of Morrison Hall at Southern Methodist University. He introduced himself and casually mentioned he was going to be a millionaire. I laughed, but I thought to myself, "Hmm . . . maybe he will be, some day."

Some people were turned off by Mark's cocky attitude. Not me. What some viewed as arrogance I saw as resoluteness. At a time when most people couldn't tell you what their major was going to be, Mark knew where he was going. He had a plan. He was smart, focused, and willing to pay the price to accomplish his dream. After graduating from college, Mark almost made his first million in real estate but was caught with a lot of properties and debt when the real estate market in Texas bottomed out. But he never went bankrupt, and the adversity was a great learning experience. Mark was disappointed and maybe even a little discouraged, but, like most successful entrepreneurs, he never lost sight of his dream.

Mark called me for lunch one day right after the downturn looking for guidance. (This is a quality all successful people have—they ask for help.) He had been thinking about going back to school to pursue a law degree. I asked him how he could afford to go to law school when he had a wife and child to support. He had already thought that through. His idea was to buy used CDs at pawnshops and sell them for half the price that record stores were charging. He had created contacts with people who owned these shops while working the real estate market. He told me that he could buy CDs for $4 and sell them for $9 at flea markets on the weekends. "People have to pay fifteen to sixteen dollars apiece in record shops," he said, "so there's a demand in the market for a lower-priced product like this."

Most people would never sacrifice like Mark, going to school full-time and working hard on weekends to pay for school and support his family. I liked the idea, and I was impressed with his level of commitment, not to mention his stamina. Mark made about $55,000 a year in the mid-1980s at flea markets on weekends working his way through law school. He not only paid for his education but also made enough money to support his family. By the time he graduated, another dream was being birthed. Mark started CD Warehouse in 1992 in a one hundred-square-foot flea market booth. That first weekend brought in sales of $3,000. Mark extended the concept into franchised retail stores that specialized in the buying, selling, and trading of used CDs. By March 2000, he had 334 stores in thirty-eight states as well as Canada, England, France, Guatemala, and Venezuela. He sold CD Warehouse, at the top of the market, for $5 million.

His next project was Movie Trading Company. Mark built on the same model he had created with the CD Warehouse concept. This time, however, he sold used movies, games, and music. He eventually sold that concept to Blockbuster Entertainment for around $12 million. How did he do it? Was it just a great idea that happened on its own? No. Was it easy? No. Nothing worthwhile ever is. By the way, he didn't succeed on his own. He had help from those closest to him. His early experience working in his dad's record shop proved to be the invaluable foundation that taught him the basic business principles that prepared him for what was to come. In fact, the key management team that helped him accomplish his dream at CD Warehouse included his dad, sister, and an old college friend, who was an accountant. They all helped the enterprise to succeed. Together they built the business up and then began to franchise it. Mark understood the importance of trusted relationships in business. He knew how to utilize his *"Who."*

WE'RE NOT DESIGNED TO "GO IT ALONE"

You're probably familiar with some of the "tongue-in-cheek" exaggerations of my dad's generation. The World War II guys would say things like "Why, when I was your age I walked three miles in the snow to school every day, and it was uphill both ways!" It was the John Wayne philosophy that said, "To truly make it in life, son, you have to go it alone." Fortunately, my dad never taught me those concepts. Yes, he did teach me the value of hard work. But he also taught me the tremendous value of teamwork, coming alongside others to accomplish a common goal. You and I need the special relationships we've been given not only to survive but thrive in this impossible world. The Bible refers to King Solomon as "the wisest man who ever lived." He said,

> *Two are better than one, because they have a good return for their work: If one falls down, his friend can help him up. But pity the man who falls and has no one to help him up.*
> —ECCLESIASTES 4:9–10

The point is clear. You need your *"Who."* Don't attempt to do life on your own. Get off the "lone ranger" treadmill. That thing will wear you out and put you in an early grave. Running faster and harder all alone is clearly not a good strategy.

The science people who study this stuff tell us that we only use a small percentage of our brainpower. The same is true when it comes to our *"Who."* Most of us haven't been taking advantage of all that's available. We're going through life with the misconception that our dreams and goals can be accomplished without any help from others. Pity the people who think they don't need coaches, teachers, mentors, parents, or friends to help and advise them. If you're among that misguided group, I've got a news flash for you: We're all *"A Cup Short!"*

Doing it your way

The song "My Way," made popular by Frank Sinatra, glorifies the philosophy of going it alone. But it's just a song. It's not real. Actually, Mr. Sinatra didn't do it his way. Paul Anka wrote the song! There was also an arranger, an orchestra and conductor, a recording studio, a sound engineer, and a record company. It was a collaborative effort. In other words, there were lots of other people involved in helping Ol' Blue Eyes do it "his way." Sinatra was a great singer and gifted performer but without the help of others we may never have heard his voice. The wise person understands that trying to go it alone is a sure way to run into insurmountable obstacles and costly mistakes!

You might be a genius in some area of your life, but you're going to need others to assist you where you're not strong. Remember, whatever it is you want to accomplish you're going to need your *"Who."* Going it alone is like trying to speed walk on the moon. It's hard to get traction. Conversely, tapping into your *"Who"* network is like walking on one of those people movers at the airport. You just step on and all of a sudden there's a power underneath transporting you to your destination faster than you could get there by yourself. Your *"Who"* friends undergird you with a power you don't have on your own. They'll ask their *"Who"* to help you get you where you want to go. They'll open doors for you that you couldn't open alone and get you connected.

If you're lost in a jungle trying to do it your way . . . STOP!

What you really need is a guide who can get you out and put you on the right path. If I was going to use a tired, old cliché right here it would be "Hey, it's a jungle out there!" But, of course, I never use clichés. I avoid them like the plague. So, instead, I'll just let you in on a basic truth about life. It's designed so that there's a built-in guarantee that you don't always get to do it your way. You're going to need some help from time to time. Your *"Who"* friends are reliable guides. So, don't waste valuable time and energy hacking your way through uncharted territory, wearing yourself out in the process. The good news is "You Got *'WHO'*!" Everyone in your *"Who"* network has their own *"Who"* network and everyone in that *"Who"* network has their circle of *"Who"* friends and on and on it goes. It's exponential!

LEAN ON YOUR *"WHO"* WHEN YOU'RE NOT STRONG

One of the greatest mistakes in business today is that most people never reach out for help, never lean on their *"Who"* in times of need. Big Mistake!

There have been many times in my life when I needed a friend to lean on. But there were many times when I chose the wrong *"Who."* Have you ever done that? Why is it that so many of us turn to the wrong people in times of need and vulnerability? Is it pride? Perhaps you're afraid that your friends will see you as weak and needy and reject you. Hey, I've got news for you. We're all weak and needy sometimes. Big Deal. The problem with that kind of thinking is that it's never true in reverse. You're a real friend to your friends. If one of them came to you for help or advice, wouldn't your heart be open to them? Of course it would! That's what friends are for. Why is it we don't want those closest to us to know we have problems? Hello! We *all* have problems! I know that, you know that, and your friends know it too. Now if you don't think you have enough real friends in your life that will help you, trust me—you do! You just have to look for them. Friends often come into our lives at just the right moment to help and encourage. I don't think that's by chance. Every significant event or milestone in your life will always involve your *"Who."* You don't have to go out and start putting it together because it's already present in your life. You just have to implement the 3 R's—Remember, Reach Out, and Reconnect.

Money, power, and fame

No one lives on this planet for very long without realizing that trouble hits from time to time. It just comes with the territory. You're going to need some encouragement, maybe a referral, an introduction, loan, or just someone to lean on. We were created and designed for relationship. Your network of friends is one of the most important components of your life. But be careful here. Don't make the mistake of thinking you need a whole new network of friends in order to be successful. Remember, *You already know everyone you need to know to get where you want to go.* If your primary goal is just gaining position, power, and money, then you're already headed in the wrong direction. If money, power, and fame were the magic bullet in life, then Elvis Presley would've been the most deliriously happy, contented person on the planet. He was extremely rich, talented, handsome, and world famous. But was he ever content or truly happy? Being at the center of your own universe isn't what life is all about. What good is it to achieve all your dreams if you're all alone?

Avoid the bunker

Unexpected change can be overwhelming. When a crisis comes, people do the craziest things. They go bonkers and begin to bunker. "Bunkering" is when you try to sneak away and hide while hoping everything will just work out. You fool yourself into believing you can manage your crisis alone. You internalize everything and shut out everyone around you. Big Mistake! That's doing exactly the opposite of what you need most. What you really need is someone who will confidentially listen, care, and help strategize with you! You need your *"Who"!* Those people who care about you and want to help . . . "just because." You need true friends who know you and can remind you how successful you've been and how your next success is "just around the corner."

Each of us has our own *"Who"* network. However, too many of us have let it slip right out of our hands. If you've allowed that to happen, you've gotta get it back! If you're going to succeed in accomplishing any goal you'll achieve it quicker and with better results when you get a little help from your friends.

Treasure hunt

Wouldn't it be tremendous to find out that the one person you need to know to accomplish a goal or fulfill your dream turns out to be a close, personal friend? Is it possible that just one positive statement or referral by a *"Who"* friend could be the key that unlocks the door allowing you to achieve an important goal? The most amazing secrets and the most profound ideas are the simplest, but a lot of times they're the hardest to see. Let me show you how I almost missed it.

I have a friend named Will who was the director of golf at

my country club. I was on the range hitting balls when we first met. We just seemed to click as friends. But when new management took over the club, all of a sudden, he was out. For the next several months Will used an office at my company to search for a new position. He eventually landed a great job in Nashville as the director of golf. About a year went by when he called and asked if we were still going to be close friends. "Of course," I said. Unfortunately, the city where he resided was not on my normal business travel route. Will told me about a special golf tournament he was invited to each year in Colorado, and he invited me along as one of his golf partners. It was a four-day event which consisted of three days of golf and a practice round. At the end of each round we would all sit around and talk. Will would always go out of his way to introduce me to every executive he knew as "the best executive recruiter in the country."

I was about to discover the hidden dynamic behind the Power of *"WHO!"* One of the people that Will introduced me to was a close personal friend of his. The introduction and endorsement was more significant to that man because of the trust he had in Will, a trust developed over many years. The man turned to me and asked, "Bob, do you, by chance, handle executive searches for CFOs?" I said, "Absolutely." He said, "Great, call me next Tuesday." It caught me off guard. I thought, "Huh? That's it?" Just Will saying I was great to one of his close friends and I land a big executive search from a major company! That one incident blew my paradigm on networking. I really never thought my golf pro friend would turn out to be a major asset to my executive-recruiting business. The idea had simply never crossed my mind. I had so compartmentalized my approach to networking that this was a real eye-opener. I'm not sure I realized until that moment that my *"Who"* friends list was quite different from all of my business acquaintances who had been acquired through years of traditional "networking." These friends could and would help me any chance they got, and I could help them. Yes, you have to be competent in your field, but you and I both know that doing our jobs isn't the tough part. Many times, it's just getting the opportunity to perform that's hard today.

It's important to note that my friendship with Will wasn't based on his position or power. It had never occurred to me that one day he might be the source of an important referral. Our friendship was based on mutual respect, interests and just plain "hitting it off." That's one of the important differences between the Power of *"WHO!"* and networking.

Principal Source of Favor

Wouldn't it be wonderful if you had a close friend, like I did with Will, who knew just the right person . . . one who already works in the world of your dream and would open the door for you? Well, that's what having favor is all about. "Favor" is simply what happens when someone you know is willing to help you accomplish things you normally couldn't do for yourself. One great adjective, a greased introduction, or a thunderous recommendation to a close friend—and guess what? You're in! End of conversation!

It's happening everywhere, every day, all around you. Just look at the political appointments, boards of directors, elite country clubs, CEO appointments, and more. Don't miss this! This is huge! Today, knowing your "principal source of favor" is of critical importance if you're going to connect with your dream, or whatever you need, for that matter. That's what *the Power of "WHO!"* is all about. It's one friend or friend of a friend who's willing to help you—just because. The "Power of Favor" is overlooked and underestimated. It can stir friends to want to solve problems on your behalf. It can get friends of friends to be sources of leads and positive references. Best of all, this kind of favor promotes a stellar reputation. Having favor in today's business marketplace is a gift that's simply beyond reason.

ANYBODY OR SOMEBODY?

Each person you already know today links you to another and another until you see the opportunity you were meant to follow and accomplish. Did you know that 80 percent of the available jobs never get advertised? Why? Because personal references from friends or friends of friends make the biggest impact on who gets the job. That's just the way it is. Now when some read this they might think, "I know what you're talking about, it's not what you know, but who you know, and who knows you." NO! That's not what I'm saying at all! It's not just any *"Who"* that will help you—it's a specific *"Who"*! The Beatles sang, "Help, I need somebody." But do you remember the next line? "Help, not just anybody."

There are several reasons you don't want to go to just *"Anybody"* to get the help you need:

■ *Anybody* doesn't really care about your dream, so don't waste your time asking them for help.

■ *Anybody* isn't reliable. They usually give advice that's convenient and helpful for them rather than useful to you.

■ *Anybody* doesn't know you personally, so they are too busy with their own agenda to stop and help you.

So, don't ask just *"Anybody"* for help. The person you want to ask is a *"Who"* friend. *"Who"* friends are not just *"Anybody,"* they're your special *"Somebody."*

■ *Somebody* really does care about you and your dream and has the power and willingness to help you.

■ *Somebody* is reliable. They are willing to take the time and effort to mentor, guide, and assist you in every way they can.

■ *Somebody* knows you personally, likes you, and will make the time to help you.

Almost everyone would agree that we all need friends! But what good is having friends if you hardly ever talk to them? So, let's take it up a notch by saying, "We need to be doing life with our friends." So start investing some time in your *"Who,"* reconnect with your *"Who,"* build your *"Who,"* nurture your *"Who,"* because in the end . . . it's all about *"Who!"* They're here to help you and you're here to help them. It just might turn out that someone you know right now will be in a position to open an important door for you later, perhaps at a time when you need it most.

From this point forward, resolve that:

■ You're going to nurture and help your *"Who"* to achieve their dreams and goals

■ You won't deprive them the joy of helping you.

YOUR *"WHO"* WORLD

Most people think networking is calling friends, family members, and business and church acquaintances and saying something like "Hey, I need your help. I'm looking for a new opportunity in this field or that. Do you know of any amazing job openings?" Often the canned response goes something like "Well, I can't think of any right now off the top of my head, but let me give it some thought, and I'll get back to you." But, of course, the call back never comes. . . .

If you want to make progress in the direction of your dreams and goals, let me encourage you to consider changing how you think about the tired, old, worn-out concept of modern networking. Networking is a misunderstood term today, because it implies friendship with people who are, in reality, only mere acquaintances. There is a better way, and that's what this chapter is all about.

Over many years working with hundreds of clients, our executive search firm developed the incredibly simple but effective networking paradigm we call the "100/40 Strategy." It's a nuts-and-bolts plan that centers networking back where it was meant to be, surrounded by one's close friends and their concentric circles of friends. It's simply a matter of focus, and I'm going to break it down for you.

INTRODUCING THE "100/40 STRATEGY"

- 1–100 = *"Who"*

- 1–40 = *"What"*

- Connecting the Dots = Success

Right up front I want to clearly define what the "100/40 Strategy" is all about.

- It's important not to get hung up on the actual numbers. It's just a term we coined, a phrase we use that describes the overall concept.

- The strategy has been time tested with phenomenal success. At the risk of its sounding like a cliché I would say it's the very reason for our firm's growth to the point of achieving national stature.

- Some say it's where "Six Degrees of Separation meets your Dream Search." But it's much more than a great business philosophy because the "100/40 Strategy" works in every area of your life. In fact, it works so well it's predictable. In other words, when you employ the "100/40 Strategy" a successful outcome is a forgone conclusion. It's that solid.

The first set of numbers (1–100) is about relationships. The second set (1–40) is about whatever it is you're after. The scale of 1–100 and 1–40 is different for every person. Anywhere along the time line of your life the number of your *"Who"* or

"What" could be radically different. But the *"Who"* part of the equation is by far the most important component. That's because whatever you truly want in life will always involve relationships. *"Who"* is preeminent!

(1–100) = *"WHO"*

Too many people start their dream search with a misstep. They focus mostly on the *"What"* (what they want) and neglect the *"Who"* (those special friends or friends of friends who can help them). There is a reason you and I have been given the friends we have, and it's this strategic group of friends that is the first part of my equation. They are the "100" in the "100/40 Strategy."

Most of us don't even think about our closest friends as possible resources when it comes to pursuing our dreams and goals. Instead, we send out form letters and résumés to strangers and pass out business cards at conferences to everyone we encounter. We tend to compartmentalize our lives into "personal" and "professional." I've seen many people make this mistake only to end up with a "job" instead of their Dream Job. Big Mistake!

What If . . . ?

■ These special friends were meant to be a lot more important to you than you had ever thought, and vice versa?

■ They were there to assist you in every phase of your life . . . physical, mental, and spiritual?

■ They were not taken for granted or compartmentalized?

■ They were meant to be your support team, your personal marketing and PR team, your financial advisers, your business and life coaches, your mentors, your personal board of directors?

■ They could have helped you in your search for your dream, or gotten you or your child into the right school, helped with finding you the right doctor, lawyer, nursing home, special tickets—you name it?

■ They were supposed to have linked and huddled with you all these years and you with them?

SPHERES OF INFLUENCE

Let's begin to go a little deeper into this simple but powerful concept. We all live in spheres. You've heard the term *sphere of influence?* A common phrase asks, "What circles do you travel in?" The fact is we live our lives in spherical worlds that touch and sometimes interconnect with the spheres of others. Most of these "contacts" are benign in nature. They're not part of your *"Who."* Your worlds touch but only in a utilitarian way. Within the bounds of normal, everyday interaction the waiter at the restaurant or the cashier at the car wash are probably not going to have any deep, personal impact on your life. By the time you get home you won't even remember their faces. We interact like this with people every day simply because we need the goods and services they provide. For the most part, it's usually a pleasant interchange but not life altering. The people I want to focus on here are the ones who do affect your life in a profound way. Because you attribute to them great value they're strategic and important to you both personally and professionally.

Life gets really exciting when it begins to dawn on you that you have some *"Who"* willing to help. Most people rarely think of their friends as conduits to achieving their dreams and goals. But friends come pre-wired with a strong desire to help us. What if they also actually had the power to cause something big to happen for us? Now wouldn't that rock your world! Maybe it's your roommate in college with whom you haven't talked in years. Maybe it's someone you worked with a long time ago who liked you then and still holds you in high esteem. But you haven't thought about them in a long time. They genuinely care about you and when you think about them now you might find yourself asking, "Why haven't I stayed in touch?"

Each person has their own special sphere of influence. When you begin to understand how this powerful dynamic works within interconnecting circles, you also begin to see how you can interact within these circles in ways that greatly benefit your life and the lives of others.

The people in your *"Who"* World are the most important people in your life because they empower you to:

- Find your purpose;

- Define your objectives;

- Reach for your dream;

- Fulfill your ambitions;

- Achieve your goals.

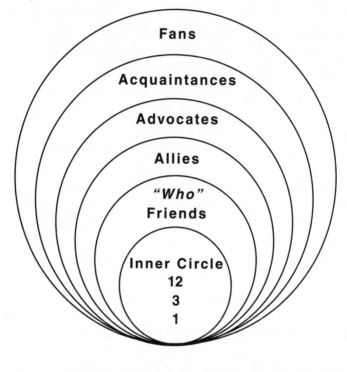

YOUR "WHO" WORLD

Your "Who" World consists of several different spheres as illustrated in the overlapping circles above. We'll begin on the inside and work our way out. As we go you will begin to recognize where certain people in your life fit in. By the time I've defined and explained each of the groups, how they function and where they fit in your life and you in theirs, you're going to have much greater clarity about who belongs where in your "Who" World.

Surprisingly, most people I talk to haven't given much thought to the varying dynamics involved in their relationships so there might be some confusion about who belongs where in your "Who" World. Each of us has been given key relationships all throughout our lives. I have broken your "Who" World into six spheres: (1) the "Inner Circle" (12–3–1),

(2) *"Who"* Friends, (3) Allies, (4) Advocates, (5) Acquaintances, and (6) Fans.

There is a "price of admission" for true friendship. Let's take a close look at each group.

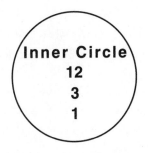

"INNER CIRCLE" 12-3-1

You get 12 friends. 3 close and 1 best.

Your closest friends are your "Inner Circle" of greatest influence. The reason so many people are confused about who their true friends are is simply because they've never declared it. If you run for office you have to declare that you're in the race. You can't be a candidate if nobody knows it. If you want to be a friend to someone, at some point you need to let them know you're in and vice versa. Friendship, by definition, involves two. You and each person in this circle have made the choice to be friends. There is a "heart connection" that you just don't have with other people. I actually call this "Your Floating 12" because rarely, if ever, will you have 12 all together in the same place at the same time. Some of your 12 live other places. You don't see them or communicate as often as you'd like. Time gets away, doesn't it? Even so, they never lose their special place in your heart. Now within this "Inner Circle" of friends there are about 3 who occupy a very present, close-up space. You may work together or your lives may be on totally different career paths but you're sharing big sections of life together. Sometimes you may get together with all 3 but most of your interaction is usually carried out on an individual basis. Although your relationship with each 1 varies greatly, these are the 3 in the inner part of your "Inner Circle." The communication level here is deeper with each 1 of these 3. But even within this close group there is usually the 1. Your best friend among your best friends is the 1 whose heart is knit to yours. There is a deep kinship that transcends even family at times.

> *Some people enter our lives and leave almost instantly. Others stay and forge such an impression on our heart and soul that we are forever changed.*
>
> —AUTHOR UNKNOWN

Have you had friends like this? Of course you have, and wasn't it extraordinary? Yes, because it's so rare to find friends like these. So when you do, you're excited and somewhat caught off guard. You're actually with someone who gets what you're all about, who just digs the way you're wired together. It's reassuring and comforting to realize there really are some people like this in your world. You're on the same wavelength. They actually like the sound of your voice. They think you're funny, witty, and wise. When you're together, life is on "enhance mode." It's very real but hard to explain. You both have the sense that you're from the same tribe. You bond at a deeper level than with your mere friendly acquaintances.

Friendships are as vital to our dreams as food and water are to our bodies. A true friend is someone who simply loves you for no good reason. They prefer you. They're always on your side. They're "true blue all the way through." An "Inner Circle" friend likes you simply because of the way you're wired together and will continue to be your friend no matter what you do. They don't need you to be anybody other than who you already are. But, at the same time, they're glad to see you become something more. Once you're aware of your dream, these friendships will act like a kind of chisel that helps you carve away everything that doesn't look like you and your dream.

However, recognizing your true authentic friends from the myriad of acquaintances that crowd around your life is difficult, because friendship has been redefined in our culture to mean something less than what it actually is.

■ Denny Crane

A poignant scene in the popular TV series *Boston Legal* succinctly captures the essence of true friendship. Denny Crane, played by William Shatner, is feeling a little insecure and doubting his friend's loyalty. Alan Shore, played by James Spader, says to his friend: "People walk around today calling everyone their best friend. The term doesn't have any real meaning anymore. Mere acquaintances are lavished with hugs and kisses upon a second or, at most, a third meeting. Birthday cards get passed around the office so everybody can scribble a snippet of sentimentality for a colleague they barely met. And everybody just loves everyone. As a result, when you tell someone you love someone today, it isn't much heard. I love you, Denny. You are my best friend. I can't imagine going through life without you as my best friend. I'm not going to kiss you, however!" These two guys are real friends, and they both know it! Do yourself an enormous favor. Don't make the potentially painful mistake of fantasizing that someone is your friend when, in fact, they are merely a friendly acquaintance. There's a few light-years' distance between "friendly" and "friend." If someone is a friend, both of you will know it, both of you will acknowledge it. It's called "declaring."

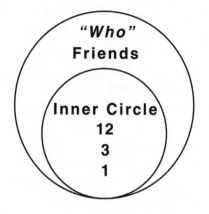

"WHO" FRIENDS

This sphere is really your "Inner Circle" expanded. Each person here shares your core values. The only factors keeping them from being a part of your "Inner Circle" are proximity, opportunity, and time. Shared experiences take all three and "Inner Circle" friends like to do things together.

One of life's pleasant little phenomena is that once someone holds a special place in your heart, they never really leave. These are friends—not acquaintances. An acquaintance who likes you will wish you well. But a friend will actually help you—starting now because they care about you. You're special to them in the same way they're special to you. They will laugh with you, cry with you, and even fight for you if need be. If you're traveling through their town, you'd rather sleep on their couch than in a king-size bed at the Hilton. Friendship has a mystical quality that you can't really explain. True friendship is based entirely on love, loyalty, and mutual regard. There are no strings attached. Your *"Who"* friends will help you—just because!

■ *Thirty-Second Voice Mail*

I have a good friend who calls me almost every day. If he doesn't get me on my cell phone immediately, he will leave me an encouraging voice mail. There have been many times when a message from him has brightened my day and caused me to smile. The message might be a quote, a cool idea, or some words from a great song. Or he might just talk about how great it is to be alive and how lucky we are to have our wives, family, and friends. You have to love people like this in a world of cynicism and negativity. Since he does this for me, I try to come up with cool things for him as well. It's become somewhat of a game we play. We try to outdo each other with encouragement. We know how tough our jobs can be sometimes, and a quick thirty-second message of encouragement at the right moment makes a real difference!

I once lost a valuable piece of business that I thought I would get. I had lost business before without letting it get to me, but this disappointment really had me bummed. I had begun to listen to the negative self-talk going on inside my head about how I could have done things differently. I was playing that old, familiar "what if" game with myself. Somewhere in the midst of this downward spiral, I checked my voice mail.

"Bob, it's Cary," said my friend. "How are you? I was just thinking of you, and I wanted to remind you how lucky we are! I ran into your wife and three daughters at the mall earlier today. Hey, man, did anyone ever tell you that you married way over your head? Those girls looked fabulous, and something else, Bob, more importantly—they looked happy. You should be so proud! Hope your business is going well today. But just in case it isn't, just remember that great things are ahead for you! So take a moment to enjoy the fact that right now you're such a blessed man. Have an awesome day!"

How do I describe the pleasure that flooded over me? His words totally transformed my entire outlook in a matter of seconds. I was inspired to "pay it forward," so I started calling several of my *"Who"* friends to give an encouraging message. Several of them called back to tell me how important and timely my message had been. Pretty soon there was a circle of encouragement going around that uplifted us all. Now before you reach for the phone and start calling people think about a couple of things: (1) Your true motivation, are you going to do this because it's in your heart to do it and you genuinely care about the individuals you're calling or are you thinking "hey, if I do this others will think well of me"? (2) Good discernment is in order. Think about how your "encouraging" call might be received on the other end. This is something you only do with your current *"Who"* friends. It's probably not appropriate for mere acquaintances.

Everyone likes to get notes of congratulations, birthday greetings, anniversary cards, etc. As you invest in your friendships, they will grow stronger and deeper. Be the kind of friend that others can lean on when they need loyalty, helpful advice, and encouragement. I want to be there for my friends. Oh, to have a friend who is there for you when your life gets all tangled up! Finding new friends is always good, but keeping the ones you have is more important. All those years of growing together, building trust, and tackling adversity together is not supposed to be thrown aside. It's one of life's extraordinary gifts to have *"Who"* friends who know you're not perfect and yet still love and accept you just the way you are. The next four spheres of your *"Who"* World are filled with the possibility of great friendship and support.

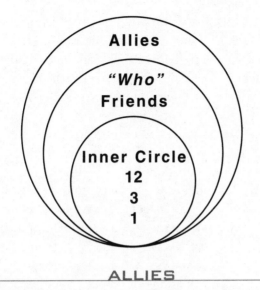

ALLIES

To associate or connect by some mutual relationship, as resemblance or friendship.

—DICTIONARY.COM

Allies are people you associate with, connect with, or touch through your 12–3–1 and *"Who"* friends. From time to time, they will introduce you to their *"Who"* friends. This is where the principle of overlapping circles comes in. Remember, we all have our own sphere of influence. When *"Who"* friends open up their world to you and invite you in, you have now been given access to a whole new group of quality people, each of whom have their own *"Who"* World. You might not get as personal as going to breakfast, lunch, or dinner with the people in your friend's *"Who"* World but you now have allies in time of need that you didn't have before just because your *"Who"* friend asks them to help you. Those overlapping circles are the Power of *"WHO!"* It's a whole different world than mere "networking."

Cheryl and my daughters are amazing, beautiful, and socially active. You can imagine how busy my house gets with all their girl friends. I gave up any illusion of being in control a long time ago. The women in my life rule my world! And I have to tell you—I love it! One day my oldest daughter, Aly, was seeking my advice on some of her goals and aspirations. It turned out to be an opportune time to review the Power of *"WHO!"* and its amazing benefits. One of her good friends, Ilana, slipped in near the end of our conversation and just listened. We had a wonderful time together and when we finished they left to go do karaoke.

Next day Aly told me about the profound effect our father-daughter talk had had on Ilana. They talked about it during the drive to the restaurant and all seemed lighthearted and fine. But as soon as they arrived and were seated Ilana broke down crying. Aly asked her what was wrong and Ilana told her, "I listened to you and your dad talk about your goals and dreams and it just hit me like a brick. As you know, Aly, my dad died a few years ago. Mom does her best to advise me but it's just not the same. This is the kind of stuff Dad and I used to talk about. Now that I've graduated this is really an important transition time in my life and I really don't have anybody to talk to about those things. I really miss my dad. I'm going to L.A. next week to look for a job. I only have one interview set up and I got that online. I'm feeling pretty lost and alone. I'm not sure it's what I want anyway. I don't know anybody and I certainly don't have any connections out there. Aly, I'm nervous. What do I do?"

Aly boldly said, "No problem . . . Power of *WHO!*"

"What?" Ilana said.

"Power of *WHO!*" Aly responded.

"What's that?" Ilana asked with a quizzical look.

"Simple," Aly said. "My dad will be your dad because I'll ask him to! Come over tomorrow. I'll set it up."

I was so proud of Aly's response! It's the essence of the movement: friends helping friends. Next day, I listened to

Ilana's goals and dreams and amazingly I had several contacts in L.A. that I knew could help her. In three short days, I was able to set her up with five interviews within her field of dreams. Of course, we bypassed the normal interviewing protocol and went straight to the top in each organization. Why? Because I was dealing with my "Who" friends. Before she went out to L.A., I called each one of them and told them about Ilana losing her dad. I told them how amazing she was and asked them if they would do me a great, personal favor. When I told them what it was, every one of my "Who" friends jumped all over it. I asked them to step in and treat Ilana like family. I knew I couldn't be there, so I asked my friends to be Mom and Dad and Sister and Brother to this wonderful young woman. My amazing "Who" friends got Ilana eight more interviews for that week she was in L.A. Ilana was stunned. She said they met her with open arms and warm hearts. She never felt like she was being interviewed. Instead it was like all they wanted to do was help. Over the next two weeks Ilana got five job offers and two of the companies were bidding on her right up until the end before she chose the one she fell in love with!

You Got "Who"! Just like Ilana. You have a circle of friends that will come to your aid in ways you never thought imaginable. It could be a neighbor, an uncle or aunt, a coach, or a friend of a friend. In the illustration of your "Who" World, I was one of Ilana's allies. She wasn't in my "Inner Circle" nor was she one of my "Who" friends. But she's in Aly's "Inner Circle." Aly knew that all she had to do was ask and her dad would help her friend. Because of Aly's "Who" I became an important ally for Ilana. Now that she's experienced, firsthand, how the Power of "WHO!" works, Ilana has become a big proponent. She's already helped many of her friends in the same way. So can you.

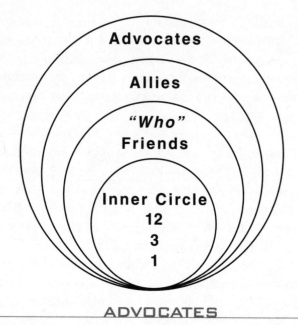

ADVOCATES

Can someone you don't even know be instrumental in helping you with your dreams and goals? Yes! Absolutely! This has to be one of life's most wonderful surprises. They're called advocates. *Dictionary.com* defines an advocate as

> {!} "A person who speaks or writes in support or defense of a person, cause, etc."

My dad often told me that help can come from mysterious places. He said sometimes people you don't even know (but who know of you) will act as advocates on your behalf. They open doors for you with a recommendation or reference. As a result you get your dream job or land a big client or get accepted into a program. An advocate can also be someone you know. You would expect a personal friend to put in a good word for you but when a stranger does it—that really gets your attention.

Several years ago I received a call from a president of a

university who told me that his athletic director, Ian McCaw, had just resigned to take a role at a bigger school and conference. Interestingly, before leaving, Ian recommended me to the president to handle the executive search for his replacement. That was quite a recommendation since it came from someone I didn't even know. The call was made even more unusual because the president wasn't asking me to come in and bid on the job. As a matter of fact, he didn't ask me anything at all about me or my firm. Not once did I have to sell myself. He was handing me the business on a silver platter based solely on the recommendation of a man he respected and trusted. If Ian said he should hire Bob Beaudine to do the search, well that's exactly what he was going to do. Our conversation lasted a shorter time than it took to write about it. It was brief and to the point. He concluded by saying he was looking forward to working with me and the check was in the mail!

I hung up the phone and leaned back in my chair. I was stunned. I remember thinking, "Is what just happened possible?" I knew I had never met Ian McCaw, so I was curious. Grateful but curious. Why would this guy do that? The following week I flew up to meet with the president. Afterward, I asked him if Ian McCaw was still on campus. The president said, "Yes, I think he's in his office over at the field house. He's going to be here for two more weeks." I excused myself and went to see Ian. I wanted to thank him for his recommendation. Even though my company, Eastman & Beaudine, was the leading sports executive search firm in the country, that was only a small part of the story. There were other firms out there with equally impressive credentials. When I asked him why he recommended someone he didn't really know he told me that he had heard me speak at a large gathering of athletic administrators. Fortunately, I must have done a good job that day because he was impressed with what I had to say and how I handled myself. My talk had made a big enough impression on him that he was willing to put his reputation on the line by recommending me to his president. I learned a great lesson that day from Ian. People are watching you. Your company's good reputation might get you in the door. But it's the personal impression you make that people remember. You could be making friends you haven't met yet. Today, Ian isn't just an advocate for me. He has moved to *"Who"* friend status. When people do nice things for you—that's a clue! I recognized it and decided to get to know Ian better. Our friendship has grown immensely and I am a better person for knowing him!

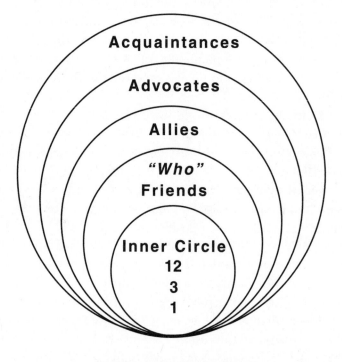

ACQUAINTANCES

Knowledge of a person acquired by a relationship less intimate than friendship.

—DICTIONARY.COM

One of the biggest mistakes people make is creating the illusion of friendship with people who are really only mere acquaintances. Nothing wrong with acquaintances. We all have them, we all need them. All friends start as acquaintances. How can you tell the difference between a friendly acquaintance and a real friend? Real friends are as different from acquaintances as diamonds are different from crystals. If you're not discerning, you will look but not see.

■ A Tale of Two Farmers

Looking without seeing was the unfortunate fault of Ali Hafed in Russell Conwell's classic story, *Acres of Diamonds*, written way back in 1843. Hafed owned a farm where he lived with his family. The land was good and filled with beautiful orchards and gardens. There was also a clear stream that contained an abundance of shimmering stones that Ali's wife used as decorative ornaments around the house. He was a wealthy and contented man until one day he was told a fascinating story that planted seeds of greed in his heart. It was about a group of people that had discovered diamonds in a faraway land. Hafed became so obsessed with the idea of finding diamonds that he could think of little else. The lightness of joy that once had graced his life began to be replaced with a heavy brooding of self-indulgence. He allowed his mind to become entirely focused on the pursuit of diamonds. Finally, driven by greed, he sold his beautiful farm, left his family behind, and went off in search of the precious gems. Hafed's quest lasted for so many years he lost all track of time. He forgot the faces of his family. Worst of all, he did not notice the change that the years had wrought in him. His lustful greed had disfigured his appearance to such an extent that even his family would not have recognized him. When the harvest of Hafed's greed came into full bloom, the magnitude of his folly was too much to bear. Overwhelmed with crushing grief, he lost all hope and took his own life.

One day the new owner of the farm happened to be crossing over a stream when suddenly he saw a sparkle of light emanating from a moss-covered stone lying in the water. Intrigued, he took it home and cleaned it up. Believing the sparkling rock to be a common crystal, he placed it on the fireplace mantel as a decoration. One day a friend from the city who just happened to be a gems dealer came to visit. When the friend walked into the living room, his eyes immediately fell upon the glittering rock sitting on the mantel. He walked closer to get a better look. Upon examination, the man exclaimed the rock was, in fact, the largest diamond he had ever seen!

"Well," the farmer said. "If you like this one, you should see the others!" "Others?" inquired the gems dealer. "Please show me what you mean."

The farmer took him to the stream where many more diamonds sparkled in the water. That farm became one of the largest diamond finds in history. Ali Hafed had ventured out to foreign lands in a vain search for what he already owned but never recognized. The treasure he sought in a faraway land was right there in his own backyard all along.

Look around the landscape of your life. Are there valuable treasures that perhaps you've been overlooking? Because diamonds seemingly last forever they're a symbol of eternity. Too often we allow the temporary to eclipse the eternal. The true and lasting treasures of life are those key relationships that have been given to us as gifts. The really scary thought is that you could be standing in the midst of your own diamond stream and not see it.

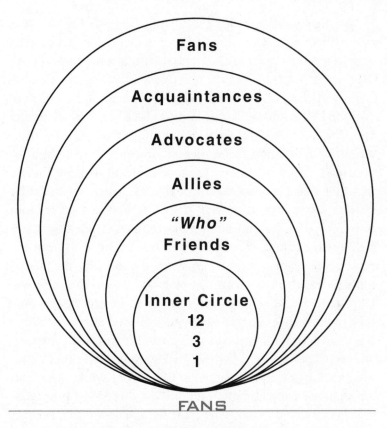

FANS

An enthusiastic devotee, follower, or admirer.

—DICTIONARY.COM

Fans are great. Major league sports could not exist without them. Entertainers could not sell their music or concert tickets without them. Theaters and broadcasters would all go dark without fans. Fans are the economic wheel that keeps things rolling. Fans fuel demand.

In the personal realm there are people who think you're great. They know of you, have encountered you professionally or socially, have read something about you, or seen you perform publicly. But fans are one degree removed. Boundaries are necessary.

Wayne Cordeiro, in his great book, *The Divine Mentor*, tells the incredible story of the giant sequoia tree that just toppled over and fell in Yosemite's National Park a few years ago. All the experts were baffled. Park rangers and forestry scientists examined the great tree for signs of damage but could find nothing that could cause such an unprecedented catastrophe. They looked closely for signs of lightning strikes, insect infestation, or mutilation from animals. Nothing! The reason for the tree's demise remained a complete mystery. How could a 240-foot tree that had been in existence since 1606 all of a sudden come crashing down? This tree had thrived for four hundred years, two hundred more than the United States itself. It was the biggest and strongest tree in the forest, the one most people came to see. It just seemed impossible that something so hugely majestic rising to the sky to meet the sun could fall overnight. Then new clues began to emerge that would take the investigation in a totally unexpected direction. When the final determination was announced it stunned everyone. We were told by the scientists that sequoias live in community. Although they are the tallest trees in the world their roots are shallow. They literally hold one another up by intertwining their roots together. This giant sequoia stood in a clearing by itself farthest away from its family root system. The clearing allowed plenty of space for spectators to congregate. It was revealed that what killed the tree was foot traffic. Over the years, visitors to the forest had so disrupted the tree's root system that it had disconnected from the life-giving flow from its neighboring trees and the tree slowly died from within. Park officials now have the oldest and largest trees protected by fences "to keep the public from trampling their root systems."

What's true of the giant sequoias is also true of you and me. We have fragile root systems. We need the protection and nurture that come from our *"Who"* friends. They are the sheltering trees who love and care for us. If you aspire to stand out in this world as an athlete, top businessperson, entertainer, or any other role in life that puts you at the top, fans will inevitably become a big part of your *"Who"* World. Remember the story of the giant sequoia that fell. One day it was there, the next day it was gone. But its demise was a long and apparently invisible process. What is true of the fences that protect the sequoias today is also true of the boundaries needed in your life that limit your exposure to fans. Too much "foot traffic" kills.

"WHAT" DO YOU WANT?

Almost every day in my recruiting practice, people call me to talk about their Dream Job. Unfortunately, what I often hear are vague generalities such as "I've always wanted to be in sports, Bob. Can you place me in one of those jobs?" My first thought is—"What job? Which sport? Do you want to be a referee, a coach, a groundskeeper, or a broadcaster?" Sports is a big field (no pun intended). Remember Tom Cruise as the sports agent in the movie *Jerry McGuire*? He made a statement that I often say to job candidates, "*You have to help me help you!*" You're going to have to be a little more specific about exactly what it is you're looking for and whether or not you're currently qualified for the position.

You may be asking, "So how do I look for it? How will I know when I find it?" Discovering your *"What"* in life is like peering through the lens of a camera while you make adjustments to bring the picture into clear focus. It's like seeing your reflection in the water after the pond becomes still. It takes a little patience. You may be one of those rare individuals who knows exactly what it is they want to do in life and you're looking for the fastest track possible to take you where you want to go. Good for you! Go for it! Let's talk. But for most people who still have a few question marks to work through there's a process involved. And this is where the dropout rate begins to go way up. I've seen it happen a thousand times. Somebody wants something, whether it's a job or some other goal. But then they find out—"It don't come easy." There's a price to pay in terms of time and effort. So, they give up. Why? Why do competent, talented individuals drop out of the process of discovering their "*What*" before they even get started? This may surprise you but one of the biggest reasons is fear. Fear of failure keeps more people stuck in the safety of the status quo than anything else. They're afraid the search will be futile. Yes, launching into the unknown can be a little scary but it's also exhilarating. You just have to keep the exhilaration from turning into anxiety. Anxiety wants you to believe your nightmares instead of your dreams. Exhilaration is energy on steroids. It's a major rush. You just have to "keep it between the ditches."

This is not only true of those seeking a Dream Job. It also applies to those seeking to achieve any goal or fulfill any aspiration.

Most people never get what they want for three simple reasons.

1. They don't ask. No one can help if they don't know what you want.

2. When they do ask, they ask the wrong people. For some reason, people are uncomfortable asking their "*Who*" for help. As a result, they'll ask most anyone except their friends, who are the only ones with a motive to help.

3. When they do ask for help, they ask too vaguely. Even if I'm motivated to help a friend, I can't do it when I don't know what he or she wants.

When you're daydreaming, where does your mind wander? Do you have a recurring dream? I've asked these questions of countless people over the years and the most common response has been "I just don't know." They go blank. Just when they need direction, purpose, and perspective, they come up empty. Too many dream seekers never decide *"What"* they want to do in life. They're bewildered by the multitude of choices that can cause them to lose hope in finding that "one thing" they were meant to do. When that happens they commit a colossal blunder. They settle for whatever comes along because it's convenient. It's the path of least resistance. Big Mistake!

It may be time to redesign your life the way you've always wanted it to be rather than living a life someone else has chosen for you. George Bernard Shaw summed it up when he wrote,

> "Take care to get what you like or you will be forced to like what you get."

FROM THE HIGH-RISE TO THE COUNTRYSIDE

A professional couple in St. Louis each made very good incomes in the corporate world. But they loved the outdoors. Every free weekend they would escape to the mountains, woods, and streams to camp, hike, fish, and canoe. This couple's dream followed the same typical pattern of most people. Work, work, work for years and years; save all the money you can, then go live the life you really want. But one glorious day they woke up and realized the years were slipping away and they probably never would have enough money to do their dream. So, what did they do? They sold their house and everything else they could and moved to Arkansas with about fifty grand in their pockets. After renting a small house, they bought a few canoes and started a rental business. As the business grew they began to build modern cabins to rent to the people who came to canoe the Buffalo River. Today, they operate one of the largest canoe rental companies in the area. Yes, they live very busy lives and work long hours. But they're not driving on freeways or working in high-rise buildings with pumped in air. If you knew this couple twenty years ago in St. Louis and saw them today in Arkansas, the first thing you would notice is they don't seem to have aged all that much.

Don't do "Dog Years." In other words, don't live one year while aging seven. Whatever you choose to do in life is going to require your time, energy, and commitment. Doing what you don't love ages you a lot more quickly. The principle is simple:

> **{ ! }** Whatever you do has a transforming effect on you. Living the life you love has the almost magical quality of keeping you young, vibrant, and healthy.

In the executive recruiting business I get the opportunity to meet and interview some of the most amazing people in the world. It's fascinating to listen to their stories of how they got from point A to point B.

Unfortunately, not all the stories have happy endings. Some describe their journey to the top as a battle. They pushed and pulled and fought to get position, power, and money only to discover that when they reached the pinnacle, it didn't satisfy and they found themselves asking, "Is that all there is?" It's been said and sung a million times because it's true, "Without Love You're Nothin'." If you have to give up love or others have to suffer so you can "make it to the top" I can tell you it's not worth it. You end up hollow. Do you really want to be like Ebenezer Scrooge? You might become stinking rich, but your life stinks. Sacrificing family and friendships to gain a few more shekels and strokes turns out to be a devil's bargain.

There's one more matter that must be taken seriously but

is often overlooked or even dismissed by many: your physical health. Are you overweight? Do you exercise regularly? Do you get regular medical checkups? Don't let something sneak up on you because you were too busy. Be sure to tend to your health. I know multimillionaires right now who would trade you their fortunes for your good health. There's no amount of money, power, or position in the world worth your health. What possible good is it to have millions in your bank account if you're not able to take a walk on the beach?

If I haven't made this crystal clear by now, please allow me to state it one more time: the core of true success is love. And that includes loving yourself enough to take care of yourself.

THE *"WHAT"* AND *"WHO"* LINK

Another reason people don't succeed in realizing their *"What"* (those hidden dreams, goals, ambitions, and purpose) is because they don't take time for reflection. Busyness can masquerade as effectiveness. When you discover *"What you want"* you get *"Who you are"* thrown in. What you truly want will derive from who you really are. In other words, it will tap into your personality, your skill set, your passion. It will fit you like a glove. You're hittin' on all eights! If it doesn't, you're missing the mark. And I don't want you to miss it. Because if you do, you run the risk of joining the ranks of all the unhappy people in the world who are stuck in a rut and dissatisfied with their lives. The important life principle here is simply, "Let *'What you want'* be an extension of *'Who you are.'*"

LOOKING WITHOUT SEEING

If your life or career becomes monotonous your head starts to tilt downward. It's unconscious. You don't even know you're doing it. There's an old adage about "keeping your nose to the grindstone." But not only is that hard on your nose, but keeping your head down prevents you from looking up. Remember, whatever you're doing—is also doing you. The law of sowing and reaping cannot be circumvented. Contrary to what you may have heard or been taught, life cannot be lived in compartments. It spills over.

You have to regularly clear your thoughts. This is best accomplished in a calm, quiet, soothing environment that inspires—a place where the constant noise of the regular world is not heard. Nature does that. Those of us who go on a Wilderness Journey discover new realities they were previously unaware even existed. Life will surprise you sometimes with something so wonderful you can't believe it. Keep looking up with an expectant, hope-filled heart and you will encounter some things that will have a deep, restorative effect.

Yogi Berra was right when he said, *"You can see a lot just by lookin'!"*

THE WILDERNESS JOURNEY

> *Your vision will become clear only when you look into your heart. . . . He who looks outside, dreams. He who looks inside, awakens.*
>
> —CARL JUNG

Railroad crossings urge you to "stop, look, and listen" before you cross the tracks. But do people heed this admonition? A lot don't. The result is a train wreck. As you begin to think about pursuing your dreams and goals, you're going to need to give yourself a "time-out." Soul searching is a solitary exercise. If you don't take this seriously you will, more than likely, settle for just another counterfeit.

A "time-out" could keep you from getting stuck for several

more years in a job that leads to another dead end. If you're not willing to pay the price for a little solitude and introspection, you will be left dealing with only surface things. By Wilderness Journey, I'm not talking about camping in a tent. Nor am I talking about taking your family to Disney World in an RV with your four kids all under the age of ten. That's called a vacation. A Wilderness Journey is something you do alone. You don't have to become a monk. (Although we can learn a lot from our monk friends about how to throttle back the RPMs of our rocket-powered lives.) A Wilderness Journey is simply a brief time away from your regular routine.

RULES OF DISENGAGEMENT

The Wilderness Journey is a time to *disengage*. Minimize distractions—anything that keeps you connected to the busyness of your normal routine. Read, walk, pray, meditate, watch a good sunset—whatever stills the pond—whatever gets you off the treadmill. Don't worry, I guarantee—it will all be there when you reengage. The goal is to quiet your mind so you can begin to think reflectively. Our noisy, high-speed, technologically advanced modern world has all but forgotten the powerful benefits of silence and solitude in nature. The familiar words of Socrates still ring true:

> "The unexamined life is not worth living."

A time of solitude and reflection creates a powerful, liberating space in which you're able to reevaluate where your gifts and talents would best be applied. When you rediscover what makes you feel fulfilled, satisfied, and content, you will have accomplished something very significant. There are millions of people who never do this, so they remain stuck where they are. They're not willing to take the risk of being alone with just their thoughts, or they don't really believe they'll discover anything new. Don't be part of that crowd. It's a dead end. Here are some important questions you will need to address during your Wilderness Journey:

■ *"What"* was it you always wanted to be growing up? Is that dream still alive in you? Is it still realistic? If not, could it be morphed into a new dream more appropriate for who and where you are today?

■ Do you have the competency, talent, or skill today to accomplish the dream? If not, can you acquire it within a reasonable time frame through additional education or training?

■ Are you where you want to be? Where you want to live? Part of the plan should be living in a place you love, in a climate that suits you, and with the friends you want to be with. Or you want to live some place where you don't yet know anybody but will have the opportunity to make new friends.

When you come to the realization of *"What you want"* to do and it lines up with *"Who you are"* as a person, then life becomes all about:

■ Doing what you *love;*

■ With those you *love;*

■ In a place you *love;*

■ That your spouse/family/mate also *loves*;

■ Doing all the above for *all the right reasons*.

GETTING OFF THE BENCH AND INTO THE GAME

I ran into one of my daughter's friends (Amy) at the grocery store. She told me she had just graduated from college. I congratulated her and asked, "So, what now?" She looked at me quizzically and said: "I have no idea. I hear the job market is bad right now, that I'd be lucky to even get a job. I'm really lost, Mr. Beaudine. I feel stuck—kind of paralyzed. Do you have any ideas?"

It's hard, if not impossible, to make good decisions when you feel that you're stuck and sinking. Amy was a student athlete in college, a 4-year starter on her Division 1A soccer team. I knew she was competitive, so I asked her what would happen if she and an opposing player were running for the ball at the same time and she didn't know what to do? What would her coach say? She laughed and said, "He would put me on the bench!" I said, "Yes, he would." All over the country, we have college students coming out of universities smart, eager, and passionate, only to find themselves headed for the bench! What a waste! If you don't know what you want to do, you need to figure it out or you run the risk of getting stuck and settling for whatever comes along. Big Mistake!

So Amy and I spent a few minutes discussing the "100/40 Strategy." These simple concepts convinced her she did, in fact, know what she loved to do, but up until now she hadn't had the time to think about it and write some ideas down on paper. She had allowed herself to become so anxious and bothered since she had come home from college that she felt paralyzed. Her mind was spinning so fast (like she had drunk two Red Bulls) that she probably wouldn't have recognized a good idea if it walked up to her and said hello. I asked her who had told her the job market was bad. "Because," I said, "It's not true." I then told her wherever she focused her job search, the energy and opportunities would begin to present themselves, and the results would follow.

All I did was open Amy's mind to the concept that her answer was probably closer than she thought. I explained she already possessed her *"Who"* made up of family, friends, coaches, and others who would be more than happy to help her find the role she desired. I simply encouraged her to get off the bench and into the game where she would discover great things, because they were already there!

Amy attacked her job search in the same manner as a college soccer game. She prepared, did her research, created a game plan, focused, and scored a job she loved!

Two weeks later I ran into Amy's mom. She told me my talk had totally turned things around. She said Amy came home energized and on a mission. She told her dad she needed a plan written down, and she needed his help. Pleasantly surprised but slightly perplexed, Amy's dad said, "That's great, honey, but didn't I already tell you that?" Sometimes we parents need other people to tell our kids the same things we've already told them. Research has shown that grown children retain only 7.9 percent of the advice offered by their parents but over 90 percent of the same advice offered by a nonparent. (Actually I just made that up, but if you're a parent, you know it's pretty close to the truth.) Hopefully this book will be a resource to remind your kids just how smart you really are!

As it turned out, Amy had a friend of the family who always liked her and wanted her to intern in a business she loved. Somehow, in all her frantic activity, Amy had forgotten about him. She also recalled a statement I made at the grocery store that day about the fact that companies look for two things from college graduates—great attitude and the willingness to put in the hours necessary to do the job well. That's why it's so important to do something you love. Otherwise, you won't be able to sustain the energy and enthusiasm required to be successful. Amy got the job because her boss already knew her and liked her. But it was her attitude and ability that moved her from being an intern to full-time employment in just two weeks.

It was easy for Amy to maintain a great attitude because all the essentials were in place:

- She loved what she was doing.

- She was working in a great environment with people she liked and genuinely cared about.

- Her family was happy and she was having a positive impact in the lives of the people around her.

- Amy's boss saw her winning attitude and the passion to give whatever time was necessary.

She was doing it for all the right reasons.

Deer in headlights

The same is true for an older, more experienced person. Don't wait for someone else to come along and make your dream suddenly appear. That's what I call "magic genie" thinking. And "genies" don't exist! Take the initiative. Develop a written plan that clearly outlines the essentials of your vision and begin to move in that direction.

One day I received a call from a friend of the family. He had been with the same company for twenty-eight years. Because of a slowdown in their industry, he was asked to take an early retirement package at age fifty-six. He was waiting for a couple of recruiters to call him back but hadn't heard from them. He joined a networking group not knowing what to expect but discovered he didn't like the experience. He described it as a group of people who had no connection, forced to sit in pairs and talk about issues and problems in each other's lives—just one notch above a sharp stick in the eye. He asked me, "Bob, what do I do? I have to work. I still have kids going to college, and one of my two girls is engaged to be married. I've forgotten how one looks for a job. It's almost like dating again, and I've forgotten how to court. I feel paralyzed." (Doesn't that sound familiar?) I asked my friend if he had developed any sort of plan. He looked at me like a calf staring at a new gate and spoke some unintelligible gibberish. Worst of all, he was actually thinking of sending out mass e-mail blasts to a bunch of people he didn't even know! He was clearly panicked. I could almost see his mind shooting out "short thoughts" like a machine gun—lots of quick bursts that spray the immediate area but lack any real accuracy. He had absolutely no clue what to do. My heart went out to this man whom I had known and respected for years. His world had been turned upside down, and he just needed a friend to put a firm hand on his shoulder and help stabilize him.

He had to calm down, take a deep breath, and begin thinking "long thoughts" like a rifle with a telescopic sight—one shot at a time that is well aimed, travels a long distance, and hits the target. Because of his panic he wasn't thinking clearly. "Long thoughts" help you focus on the essentials. By the way, my friend looked around and discovered a franchise opportunity through one of his *"Who"* friends. He is now more successful than he ever was in his previous job and in control of his own destiny.

DREAMING OUT LOUD— THE "40 LIST"

The next step is to come up with a list of your dreams, goals, and aspirations. This is the second piece of the "100/40 Strategy"—the "40 List." It's the *"What you want to do and accomplish in life list."*

It's important to write it down, put it up on a "dream wall" so you and your *"Who"* World can see it and then begin to "dream out loud" how you're going to get it. A "dream wall" needs to be on a changeable surface like a chalkboard or one of those cork bulletin boards you can pin things to. A good "dream wall" would be one of those white surface boards or dry erase boards that you can draw on with multicolored markers.

What I love about a "40 List" is that it's an inventory tool, a simple to-do list that will act as a daily reminder for whatever it is you want to reach, achieve, accomplish, or fulfill. Nothing's more impressive today than talking to people who know who they are, have done their research, and know exactly what they want to do in life. They're more knowledgeable about where they want to go, they're focused, and they bring passion to their pitch. It's almost as if they're calling something that's not as though it already is. This is a great style to embrace! In real estate, it's all about location, location, location. When pursuing dreams and goals, it's all about preparation, preparation, preparation.

Now you'll be pleased to learn, that no matter *"What"* it is you're seeking, someone has already done the "research" you require. Today there is a directory for almost everything. The company or organization you're seeking is probably part of an association, and again there is lots of important *"Who"* information you'll need right there on the Web. Use these outlets as a starting place. Then follow up with specific companies and organizations or refer to their Web sites to correctly identify the "person" to whom you would report/need to contact in each of the "40." Don't forget, when doing *"What"* research, the ultimate goal is to identify the specific names of the people you'll need to know so you can review them with your *"Who"* friends!

Note: If you have an entrepreneurial mind-set and your dream is to start your own company, you'll still need a "List" of people to assist you. Your list could include venture capital companies, banks, funds, wealthy individuals, or foundations. You'll need partners, mentors, board of directors, and staff. Take the initiative. Start digging. People will be more willing to assist you if they know you've done your research.

Why "40"?

So what's the importance of coming up with 1 to 40 names? Is there something unique about the "40" portion of this strategy? Once again, it's important not to get hung up on the actual number. But the "magic" of this approach is that it's the number of organizations and people you can embrace effectively in networking forward. For most folks, just being out of work (or stuck in a job you dislike) is extremely stressful. The "networking" process becomes more stressful if you have just a few names on your list and they haven't called you back.

But I've often heard people say, "I'm not sure I know forty possibilities." Sure you do. Let me show you one example. Let's say you wanted to tie your two loves together—public relations and sports. Well, your "40 List" list could include teams, league opportunities, universities, sporting goods manufacturers, Olympic bodies, major PR agencies, stadiums/arenas, etc. Every industry has a multitude of employment choices to consider. Whether it's arts, transportation, entertainment, sports, consumer package goods, oil and gas, technology, or medical—you need a list. Once you have one, you need to write down all these possibilities so you can see them. Football and basketball coaches will always tell you:

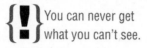 You can never get what you can't see.

That's why they have playbooks and put all the possible plays on the quarterback's forearm so he won't forget. Basketball coaches do the same. They have a small chalkboard courtside that they use at time outs to diagram exactly the play they want to run. This allows each player to *see* exactly what they are to do. It's a visual thing. The same is needed for dreams and goals, and that's why you need a "List" you can *see*.

CONNECTING THE DOTS = SUCCESS

It's so much easier for your "Who" World to assist you if you've done some research and can review even a few specific names (1–40) of organizations and people you want to know. The good news is that I'm not asking you to make cold calls; I'm just asking you to call your friends, so relax. Friends love to give career advice and are flattered when you ask them for help, so don't be shy. With "Who" friends, you don't have to validate your credentials; just ask for their assistance.

Don't be concerned if your friends don't know the specific names you're asking about from your "40 List" because, in fact, it really doesn't matter. If they don't recognize the names on your list, they'll begin to feel uncomfortable about not being of assistance and will want to help in some other way. After all, they're your "Who." Ideally, you'll wind up with at least one key name in an organization similar to one on your "List." One personal friend of theirs whom they have known for years (one of *their* "100 List") will help get you going in the right direction.

You may be asking, "But what if I don't get a name from each person on my (1–100) list?" Well, the odds are in your favor: 100 friends x 40 opportunities = 4,000 potential hits . . . you only need 1!

One final note here: Even if a particular *"Who"* friend can't offer you a single name, listen clearly to what they have to say. Be receptive to their ideas and suggestions. It's very important to have your "radar" on in conversations like these. Your *"Who"* friend might not know the specifics concerning your dreams and goals but may offer a different perspective that could prove to be invaluable. So, take off the blinders. The answer to your dreams and goals could be hidden in one of these conversations.

Unfortunately, many people are reluctant about making a list because they think it backs them into a corner. That's precisely the point! It absolutely does! A list is ruthless because it makes you be specific about *"what you want and don't want."* A menu in a restaurant lets you know what it offers, but it also lets you know what it doesn't. A list helps you to say yes when you need to say yes and no when you need to say no. If you don't know your true desires, someone or something could appear right in front of you, and you wouldn't even recognize the opportunity. A list creates accountability because you will have to let some things go in order to pursue what's on your list. A list acts like a kind of menu for your life. Let's look deeper at this concept of a list.

LISTS AND INSTRUCTIONS ARE NOT YOUR ENEMY

I'm making a list and checking it twice.

—SANTA CLAUS

A strong case could be made about the importance lists have played in the history of the world. Moses got the all-time "Top 10 list" from God on Mt. Sinai. The Bill of Rights is the foundational list of protections we enjoy as U.S. citizens. Every year *Fortune* magazine publishes its list of the top five hundred companies in the world. Kids of all ages make up their Christmas wish lists every year. Without a list, I'd be lost at the grocery store. Now, there's even the *Book of Lists* to help us keep track of all the lists. The list could go on but . . . (Sorry, that was just too tempting.) Lists create structure and bring clarity. I once made a list that changed my life. It came about as a result of a growing emptiness inside. The emptiness took on a voice and started speaking to me. No, I wasn't hearing actual voices. It was much louder than that.

THE LIST

I was twenty-seven years old when I began to seriously think about a wife. I had spent a lot of time and energy doing what Johnny Lee sings about, "Looking for love in all the wrong places." Slowly, I began to realize that I was probably going to have to make some fundamental changes in my life. I had just moved back to Dallas and was attending a new church. The pastor was away traveling overseas, and a visiting speaker from New Zealand, Donald Crosbie, gave a great message that really inspired me. After the service I went up to introduce myself and tell him how much I enjoyed his talk. He appreciated my words of encouragement, and we struck up a friendship. Much to my surprise and delight, Donald was speaking again the following Sunday and delivered another inspiring talk. I couldn't resist the urge to approach him once again and tell him how much I enjoyed his talk. He and his wife invited me to join them for lunch, and I eagerly accepted.

During our meal we engaged in a lively discussion about many things, punctuated by personal anecdotes and lots of laughter about our lives. Donald's wife, Valmae, asked me if I was dating anyone seriously. Like most single guys that age, I got that question a lot. When I said no, they looked at each other and smiled. It was as if they knew something I didn't. Their conversation became animated as they began telling me about a young lady they felt was the perfect match for me. Perfect match? Were they kidding? How could they possibly know what a perfect match for me would be? They had just met me! But they were confident and continued, convinced that what they were sensing had a divine origin.

Donald began to describe a beautiful young lady named Cheryl who had something important in common with me that only they knew about. Intrigued and slightly curious, I asked him to explain why they felt so strongly about this. He said that over the past two weeks, Cheryl and I were the only ones in the entire congregation who had approached him after the service to encourage him about his talks. I thought about the odds of that and had to admit it did seem a bit unusual that, out of a crowd of a thousand people, only two of us had spoken to him about his message.

"Bob," he said, "I want you and Cheryl to meet. We're hosting a covered-dish party at our house next Saturday." "Wait a minute," I thought, "a what? I'm twenty-seven years old, an SMU graduate, and basically a pretty cool, hip kind of guy and you want me to meet a girl at a covered-dish party?" Visions started forming in my head of a bunch of middle-aged married couples gathering in an overcrowded room along with Aunt Bea and Grandpa. Sensing my reluctance, he said something that has stayed with me my entire life.

"Bob, if you want to have something that you've never had before, you've got to be willing to do something that you've never done before!" He got me there. I couldn't help but think this may have something to do with some of those foundational changes I wanted to make in my life.

All week long I thought about the upcoming party. I started talking to myself, "Maybe I just don't show up. I could always go to another church. It's not like they have my phone number or know where I live. What if their idea of the 'perfect mate' for me is very different from mine? What if this girl Cheryl turns out to be the 'church lady'? Oh no, what have I gotten myself into? Well, he did say she was beautiful and, after all, his wife is a knockout. Okay, okay, I'll go, but if I don't like it, I'll just turn on the Beaudine charm, be very polite to everybody, and check out the first chance I get."

When I arrived I parked my car several houses down the block. If I had to make a run for it, I wouldn't get stuck talking to someone right in front of the house. It was much easier to make a quick exit, turn, and just keep walking. I had learned over my bachelor years that a good exit strategy is essential. As

I entered the house, Donald spotted me immediately and came right over with a hearty handshake. He wasted no time in pointing me toward the kitchen. "Bob," he said, "there's Cheryl." Standing in front of me just a few feet away was a small group of women, maybe five or six. I quickly scanned each one of them and felt a panic in the pit of my stomach. A prayer formed on my lips, "Please, God, if you're listening, let it be the one on the right." Donald escorted me into the kitchen, and when he called out her name Cheryl turned toward us. She was the one on the right! I was relieved and elated all at the same time. She was everything Donald and Valmae had said she was—and more! She was drop-dead gorgeous, a slender blonde with beautiful, bright eyes that lit up the whole room when she smiled. Cheryl extended her hand and said, "Hello, Bob, nice to meet you."

After talking for a while, we walked out of the kitchen and found a semiprivate corner where our discussion continued for the next two to three hours. I don't think we took our eyes off each other during the entire evening. It was pretty obvious the sparks were flying. Being an executive recruiter, I was employing all my interview skills. However, she possessed some formidable interview skills of her own. We found out as much as we could about each other in one evening, and I knew I wanted this to continue. The hour was getting late, so I asked her out for the following night, and she accepted.

About three weeks into our developing relationship, I drove over to pick her up at her apartment for our fifth date. We were going out to dinner with another couple, and they were running a few minutes late. As we sat on the couch making small talk, Cheryl shifted her body to look directly at me and asked, "Where is this going?" Being a little slow on the uptake, I answered, "Where's what going?"

"Are we just casually dating, or is this something more?"

"Oh. I think this is something more," I replied.

She asked, "How would you know?"

Without even thinking I blurted out, "Because I have a list." As soon as I said it, I thought, "Uh-oh, now she's going to think I'm weird."

"What do you mean you have a list? What list?"

I couldn't turn back now, so I told her, "I made a list about four months ago outlining everything I was looking for in a serious relationship." At that moment Cheryl looked away, staring across the room. I thought, "Oh no, she probably thinks I'm nuts."

When she looked back at me I could see the stunned expression on her face as she blurted out, "Four months ago I made a list of what I was looking for in a man." Now we were both stunned. We blurted out almost simultaneously, "Go get your list!"

I drove as fast as I could and made it back just as our friends were arriving to go out for the evening. So, we postponed our "list comparison session" to later that night when we could be alone. After a terrific dinner, we said goodnight to the other couple and headed back to Cheryl's apartment. We began to share our lists and were astonished to discover that we fit each other perfectly. There were even some amazing details, the odds of which are astronomical. She wanted her man to be in a family business so there could be flexibility (I worked with my dad in executive recruiting). I wanted her family to have land (her father owns a sizable ranch). Both of us wanted parents who were still married (each of ours had been married for over thirty years). Both of us wanted our families to live in Texas. Both of us wanted a college graduate for a mate. Our lists contained detailed information outlining physical preferences like height and other attributes. Both our lists were very specific on matters of faith, number of children, and a love for music and sports. We also each desired a mate who would be athletic and love to dance and travel. Our lists went on for three pages! We wrote about the importance of communication and conversation in a lifelong relationship. The most important wish on each of our lists was the desire that our mate be our best friend.

It should be no surprise to you that one of my favorite songs from the 1980s is Hall and Oates's "Your Kiss Is On My List." Cheryl and I dated for only three months before I asked her to marry me. I'm very happy and grateful to tell you that I'm more in love with Cheryl today after twenty-five years of marriage.

I told you this personal story about Cheryl and me because I believe that the quest for the perfect mate and the search for your dreams and goals are very similar in one important aspect: both require a list of specifics outlining what really matters to you. If you don't know what you want, you'll get it. The great thing about a list is that it really helps you clarify your priorities, your values, and your personal preferences. In short, making a list helps you dream. Dreaming out loud is what lists are all about. You think about it, you begin to speak about it, and you write it down.

THE INSTRUCTIONS

I want to give you *four* instructions you'll need to make a *good* list to help you chart your future course. Making a list is relatively easy. Making a *good* list, however, requires something more. You will have a good list when you dream it, believe it, and have confidence in it. Only then will you be able to do it!

1. *Dream It*

One of the key components of dreaming is the ability to allow yourself to drift a little, kind of like sailing. One of the joys of sailing is getting out on the water on a beautiful day, hoisting the sails, and letting the breeze take you where it will. There's an exhilarating sense of adventure in not knowing exactly where you're going. Dreaming is letting your imagination out into the wind a bit. Not a whirlwind, but certainly a strong enough breeze to take you where you begin to see new possibilities that you haven't seen before. When you're dreaming there can be a kaleidoscope of various thoughts and images. Along the way, however, something will begin to stand out that holds your attention. You've just connected with your desire. Desire is something you enjoy. You easily fix your mind on it. Remember, you will never be successful at something you don't enjoy.

When he was a very young man, Winston Churchill had a dream that one day England would come into extreme danger and he would be called upon to save the day. From time to time he would tell some of his friends about the dream but was often told that his dream was childish, something akin to a superhero comic book. The future prime minister would reply, *"I believe in destiny, and when destiny calls you must obey."*

I would add that Mr. Churchill's destiny was speaking to him in his recurring dream, helping to guide him and prepare him for what was to come. It wasn't until the final season of his life that the dream became a reality. When Hitler's Nazi Germany attacked England, Churchill did, indeed, save the day. Most successful people will tell you they always thought they would be successful. They will tell you they heard the voice of their destiny calling to them, and they answered.

I cannot impress upon you strongly enough the vital importance of keeping a journal of the pursuit of your dreams and goals. Even if you make an entry only once every few days, a journal will be your most valuable ally in recognizing the patterns of your life. Patterns reveal destiny. If you've ever watched a *Star Trek* episode on TV you've probably noticed that at the end of each program Captain Kirk records a spoken entry into the ship's log. He begins by announcing the "Stardate." What follows is a synopsis of events that took place during the episode and how things were resolved. A journal is your "ship's log." It gives you a picture of where you've been and what you've been doing. It will give you great insight into determining your future direction. And with today's technology it's easy to keep an audio log.

You draw conclusions by listening to and trusting your instincts. Daydreaming is important. Some people may think it silly, but what may appear, at first, to be inconsequential musings often lead to much grander concepts. Ask any successful writer, architect, or detective. You've heard it a thousand times—"One thing leads to another." It's true, so write down what you've been dreaming about along with events that take place in your life, even if it's just a sentence or two every few days. Your daydreams could be messages calling to you from your destiny.

2. *Believe It*

Belief means having the confidence that what may not be readily apparent in objective reality actually already exists. Columbus believed the world was round when everybody else thought it was flat, a farmer believes the seeds he plants in the ground will yield a bountiful crop. In the same way, you must believe that the seeds you sow will reap a harvest.

I sat in my office one night thinking to myself, "Now that I've done a lot of work for universities successfully placing athletic directors, what else could I do in that industry?" The thought just popped into my head, "How about placing coaches?" I got chills thinking about it. I always wanted to place coaches. "Hmm . . . but how do I get that kind of search when I've never done one before?" The next thought that came to my mind was "If you want something you've never had, you have to do something you've never done. Well, I've never created a brochure about placing coaches, so I think I'll start there."

I thought through all the needs an athletic director would

have doing a coach search and tried to put myself in their shoes so I could better understand how to be the solution to their problems. I wanted to customize a solution to what the athletic director needed, so I called several AD ("*Who*") friends I had already placed seeking their counsel. It was time very well spent. What I learned is there is a step-by-step process in hiring a coach that can be like walking through a minefield. One misstep and the whole thing blows up in your face. First, I would have to convince the AD that I understood every aspect of the process and the pitfalls along the way. Next, I would have to demonstrate I could effectively and confidentially manage the search while protecting the school during the process. If I could create a comprehensive solution, in writing, that would make the search for a coach easier for the athletic director, I'd be in business. I worked and worked on the brochure for a solid week. I was calling things that are not as though they were. There was no actual business in sight. All I had was a clue and a passion. I finished the brochure at 7:15 p.m. on a Friday. As I was leaving the office, the phone rang. It was an AD friend asking if I could recommend someone to help with his search for a new coach. I almost dropped the phone! I said, "Yeah, me!" His response was tentative, "Bob, I wasn't aware you did coach searches. Do you have anything you could send me that I could review with my president?" "Hold on," I said, and I e-mailed the brochure I had finished just minutes before.

Can you believe it?! When he opened his e-mail, he loved it, and within twenty-four hours I was hired! Over the next four years, I personally conducted over twenty successful head coach searches in basketball and football. All because I followed my initial instincts to create that brochure even when there was yet no search in sight! Follow your dream. Act on it in faith! You must believe!

3. *Have Confidence in It*

Did you ever have to make up your mind?

Decisions! Decisions! Decisions! When someone says "Stop, world . . . I want to get off," what they're really saying is that life would be easier if they didn't have to make so many decisions. One of life's great paradoxes is that by not deciding, you're making a decision. If you don't decide who and what you want to be or are not willing to pay the price to get there, then somebody else will handle those things for you. If you're fulfilled and happy in your current circumstances, then you decide that, as far as you're concerned, you will remain where you are. The same exact principle applies in the reverse. Of course, I'm not telling you anything you don't already know. The greatest limits in life are not external but internal. Every invention, song, or work of art started as a seed of an idea that took dedication and effort to bring into objective reality. Like the book you're now reading or the CD you listened to recently, somebody was inspired with an idea that became a dream that took a lot of work to make real. All over the country, people are not being decisive. They're "fence-sitters." They are waiting for someone else to give them direction.

I received a phone call from a casual acquaintance who is the CEO of a major corporation. I could tell from the tone in his voice that he needed my full attention. He said he was about to go into a board meeting and wanted to know if he should be confident in aggressively telling the board the direction he felt the company should go. His concern was that if the board didn't like his ideas, he might lose his job. He wanted to know how he would be viewed in the job market if he got canned. After listening to his story, I answered, "You're the CEO. It's your duty to tell the board your plan. How you tell the story of your plan is the crucial part. Presentation is everything. If you're fully prepared when you walk in the room and confident enough to answer any questions or challenges, you'll win. If not, it won't work anyway. So be yourself. You have a great track record and an excellent record of achievement. Don't allow any negative self-talk to hinder you. Go get 'em!"

Well, the board loved his ideas, the company has prospered, and so has he. Being prepared and confident causes others to feel comfortable with your leadership. Being resolute and courageous in the execution of your list is crucial for success. The choice of what will happen to you is the result of all the little decisions you make every day. So, make the best possible decisions today, and tomorrow will arrive smiling at you. You're not yet what you will become. The only way to get there is to be the best version of yourself today!

4. *Do It*

Nike's slogan has become part of the fabric of our culture. "Just Do It" seems sparse in its austere simplicity, but behind its profound wisdom is the stuff dreams are made of. There's a time to stop thinking about it; you'll never see all the angles. There's a time to stop preparing; too much knowledge can bog you down. Yes, there is even a time to stop hoping for it; at some point you have to get off your butt and launch! You have to act! You have to step out!

What if the two bicycle mechanics from Dayton, Ohio, had never made that long, arduous trip to Kitty Hawk, North Carolina? What if they just dreamed about flying but never acted on their dream, never ventured beyond their bike shop? What if Orville and Wilbur had spent all their time talking about the concepts and theories of flight instead of building that awkward, gangly contraption that actually flew for twelve seconds and changed the world by giving mankind the gift of flight?

Without action, all great ideas are useless. There is no shortage of great ideas. The key that turns dreams into reality is a good plan of action. The people who act on their ideas are in the minority. Successful people share *five* simple but important traits that all dream seekers can use.

IMPORTANT TRAITS OF SUCCESSFUL PEOPLE

1. *They Start*

An old Chinese proverb says, "Be first to the field, last to the couch." Here's another good one to remember: "Yard by yard, life is hard; inch by inch, it's a cinch." It may sound trite, but it's true. You don't have to make a big splash. You don't have to call a press conference. Just begin. If you have a dream, it's going to take some creative thinking, strategizing, and good, old-fashioned hard work to bring it into reality. Set your course then stick to it even in the face of adversity or setback. Don't wait for some great benefactor to recognize your genius or talent and begin to fund and promote you. If you do, you'll likely be waiting your entire life. That's exactly what a lot of people do. Someone who dreams of becoming a famous actor but never goes to acting school or tries out for a part is only fantasizing, not dreaming. Dreams are something you act on. President Franklin D. Roosevelt said, "It is common sense to take a method and try it: If it fails, admit it frankly, and try another. But above all, *try something*!" I'm amazed so many people will continue to do the same things that don't work for them and never try something new.

The idea that you could begin right now to launch out into deeper water and make a move toward your dream is exciting.

2. *They Are Not Discouraged by Obstacles*

What others see as an impassable mountain, dreamers see as merely a big rock in the way. It's simply something that must be dealt with. Yes, it may take some time and effort, but dreamers consider this just part of the process of getting where they need to go.

Obstacles should be viewed as springboards to bigger and better opportunities. Your friends and mentors can help launch you over some of those barriers by providing powerful leverage that you don't have on your own. That's where the "100/40 Strategy" works so beautifully. It tells you that the odds are that someone you know right now knows another person who can provide a better and more creative solution to your situation, a way to circumvent your obstacle. There's no embarrassment in asking for help. In fact, it's just plain smart. Remember, one slight change in strategy could mean huge success, whereas no change or standing still will not accomplish anything.

3. *They Turn Mistakes and So-Called Failures into Stunning Success*

Failure is not fatal, but failure to change might be.
—COACH JOHN WOODEN

People are too concerned about making mistakes, and this fear of failure causes them to become stuck. In other words, they don't even try anymore. Remember, "Failure is an event, not a person," as my Plano, Texas, neighbor Zig Ziglar says. "It's just an experience where we didn't like the result." What I've discovered in the executive search business is that failure is overrated. If viewed correctly, it just provides real-life instruction/training and another chance to experience success. You can strike out over and over, each time slightly changing your strategy, when all of a sudden, you find that "sweet spot." During his era, Babe Ruth was the all-time home run king. But he was also baseball's all-time strikeout king. The point is, he never stopped swinging, always looking for that "sweet spot."

Let me tell you about one of the most unforgettable business trips of my life. I was working out in the hotel gym when Tom Selleck came in. He is one of my favorite actors. I loved him in *Magnum P.I.* I was on a bike and he jumped on one next to mine. I wasn't going to say anything to him—just let him have his quiet workout time but he started a conversation with me. He was interested in my job, my family, my life. He was just a good guy wanting to pass some time while riding the bike! He loved the fact that I did sports recruiting. He was a really good athlete himself in baseball and volleyball. He told me he had initially wanted to be an architect but stumbled on to modeling and acting. The conversation came around to how hard it was to get a break in that business. He said it had taken years and years of acting classes, workshops, and summer stock, but he loved all the work. Friends and family, of course, questioned his choice, after so many rejections, because he was too tall, had the wrong look, was too good-looking, etc. It was always "not this, not that." I told him it was the same in the business world and asked how he stayed the course through all the so-called failures. Why hadn't he quit?

"It's all here between the ears," he said. "You have to decide to follow your dream, commit, and, most of all, turn so-called failures into successes. In one moment it happened for me. I got the part in *Magnum P.I.*, and the rest is history. All those years being hungry, practicing persistence, and believing this is what I was supposed to do paid off, I guess."

The school of hard knocks, whether in business, politics, sports, or entertainment, should be viewed as just another method to test your coolest and craziest "knockout ideas." You work and work and work until it works for you. The "best of the best" never run from failure; they analyze the causes and make sure mistakes aren't repeated. We all make mistakes and experience setbacks. How you respond to these bumps in the road is everything!

4. *They Maintain Self-Discipline*

The person who writes a book understands that you don't quit your job, take six months out of your life, and go to a secluded island somewhere to do it. Instead, these doers of dreams have figured out that a book is written one page at a time, so they chip away at it, a little every day or every other day until it's finished. John Grisham dreamed of becoming an author. His first book took three years to write because he was working full-time in a law firm. But he had the discipline, born of a joyful desire, to work at it an hour at a time. Today, he is considered one of the most prolific and successful authors of all time. Now he can buy his own secluded island!

5. *They Stick to It*

The amazing minority of people who are successful dreamers realize that their dreams are not going to happen overnight. If you believe that dreams just come true on their own, perhaps you should buy some lottery tickets. It's an all too common fact that most people just give up too soon. They meet with some adversity, allow themselves to become discouraged, and give up, convinced that their particular dream is not worth the effort or is just not meant to be. Big Mistake! Proactively working toward achieving a dream is a process of trial and error, setbacks and dead ends, disappointments and discoveries. That's why the dream you choose to follow has to be its own reward. Your dream must be something that has the power to keep you motivated and in pursuit no matter what, because no matter what you'll have to persevere.

Wearing those old-time knickers, his fist pumping forward and leg in the air, Payne Stewart, one of golf's greatest players, thrilled fans at the U.S. Open back in 1999 as the final winning putt rolled into the cup. But the road that led to winning that major championship was a rough one. During his career there were a lot of missed cuts, second-place finishes, and complete collapses (it happens to all of us, doesn't it?). One year while playing in front of his hometown Dallas crowd and SMU friends at the Byron Nelson Classic, he blew it and lost the tournament on the first play-off hole. His face told the whole story. I could tell he felt he had let everyone down (and you thought you were the only one who ever felt that way). We all watched him walk off hand in hand with his wife, Tracy, back to the clubhouse. It was a long and lonely walk for both of them. No cheering crowd, no standing ovation, just a small group of reporters waiting to pepper him with questions about the loss. But did Payne quit? Of course not! There was no *quit* in him. Don't let there be any in you, either.

LIFE PROVIDES CLUES

*Eliminate all other factors, and the one which
remains must be the truth.*

—SHERLOCK HOLMES

herlock Holmes became world famous for his uncanny ability to perceive clues. He saw what others
couldn't until he pointed them out. This remarkable gift of
"seeing" most often revealed clues hidden in plain sight. You
and I need the ability to detect the clues life sets before us.
They're actually easy to see, but, as you and I know, we often
miss the obvious.

A LASTING LEGACY

David was in near despair as he was driving home in Chicago.
He had just finished an interview for a job he really wanted,
but he knew the interview hadn't gone well. With no other
prospects in sight, he was feeling like dust on an empty shelf.
Earlier that day, David had told his wife he felt certain he
would get the job because of his qualifications. Both their
hopes were high. The thought of facing her now with what he
knew was another defeat was almost more than he could bear.

Distractedly, he turned on the car radio to get his mind off his dilemma. He had no way of knowing he was about to have a life-changing encounter. After pushing a few buttons he came across an interview program that caught his ear. The host was talking with the author of a book titled *Ultimate Success*. The writer's name was Frank Beaudine from Plano, Texas. David was transfixed by his deep, resonant voice. It actually made the speakers vibrate. He had never heard a voice quite like that, and it seemed that Mr. Beaudine was speaking directly to him. The interview lasted only five minutes but left an indelible mark on David.

The last question the interviewer asked was "Mr. Beaudine, is there any advice you can offer that might be helpful to the person listening right now who is out of work, exhausted by all the rejections, and starting to lose hope?" "This is incredible," David thought. "Do these people know me?" He leaned into the radio, not believing what he was hearing. Frank Beaudine's answer came like distant rolling thunder from heaven, "You might have just bombed your last interview, but don't despair. Something great is just around the corner."

David's eyes widened, and his mouth dropped open. What were the odds of hearing exactly what he needed to hear at exactly that moment? David would tell you it was divine providence.

Clues can appear in unlikely places and come from unexpected sources. In David's case the clues he needed showed up on his radio from a total stranger as he listened to an interview program. In just a few short minutes he went from feeling utter defeat to gaining the encouragement he needed that catapulted him into his Dream Job on his very next interview. But that's not the end of the story.

It's now seven years later and it's been six months since my dad passed away. The cards, flowers, and phone calls were fading memories. So, imagine my surprise when a call came from a man wishing to speak with my dad. Intrigued by who the caller might be, I reached for the phone thinking, "It's probably an old friend who just heard the news."

It was David, the radio listener from Chicago. I informed him that my father had passed away. The silence on the other end of the line told me he was shocked and saddened by the news. He apologized for not knowing, but I told him I was glad and grateful that someone was still thinking about my dad! That seemed to put him at ease, and he began telling me the story about that drive home seven years before in Chicago. He said that when the interview was over, my dad offered to give a copy of his book to the first ten people who called his office.

Interestingly, David was the only one who called that day. He told me, "Your dad's book made a significant difference in my life and my marriage. Today, I'm successful beyond my dreams. I'm Senior VP of a major consumer packaged-goods company. I've often thought about your dad over the years and how the radio interview and his book changed my life. I found his phone number in my wallet today and decided I would call and say thank you. I'm so sorry I'm too late."

I replied, "No, David, your timing is perfect. My mom will be so happy to hear you speak of my dad and the impact he and his book had on you. Your call today will bring her great joy!"

My dad was truly a great encourager. He was the one who first taught me about the principles I am now teaching you in this book. Sir Isaac Newton, when publicly praised for a lifetime of great accomplishments, replied by assigning the credit to his predecessors, "If I have seen further than other men, it's only because I have stood upon the shoulders of giants." My dad was a giant who knew all about the Power of *"WHO!"* and I am glad I get to pass on his legacy to you.

Regaining equilibrium

Anyone on a great quest is looking for clues that will help guide them. David's story is a common one played out in the lives of people every day all over the world. You're headed in the right direction, fully confident that everything is going fine when, suddenly and without warning, your world gets turned upside down. It can feel like walking off the edge of a cliff in the dark. One moment you're on solid ground. Next, you feel like you're free-falling upside down. Your heart is in your stomach. Instinctively, your arms reach out, flailing around for anything you can grasp that will stop your fall. In real life, beware of grabbing onto the first thing that comes along. Gifted individuals who temporarily lose their confidence can do some really stupid things. The first job that comes along might look like your salvation but could turn out to be just another detour that leads you away from your dream. Panic is a major cause of forgetfulness and temporary blindness. When you feel like you're in a free fall, it's hard to remember who you are, much less what you should do next. So, I'm going to tell you. Look for the clues. You have to look for them because they can be subtle, blending in with the landscape of your life like a camouflaged animal lying in the brush. These clues can be right in front of you but you still don't see them. Here's a tip. Don't squint. Don't use a magnifying glass. Relax your mind's eye and just begin to look around.

Here are the *five* clues you're looking for.

Clue 1.—The recurring dream

Each of us has an assignment, a purpose, a dream all our own that we need to discover or rediscover. Maybe you've wanted to open a restaurant, become a fashion model, get your real estate license, or go back to law school. It's always been there and keeps resurfacing. Your dream is unique to you, and the fact that you still have this dream should speak loudly to you. That's your first clue. But in order to see the next step, you're going to have to disconnect from some of the old patterns of your lifestyle.

Neo is the main character in the movie, *The Matrix*. He's connected to the "grid," unaware that he's going through life asleep. After being awakened and disconnected from the "grid" through a bizarre set of circumstances, he's faced with a whole new reality that he didn't even know existed before. This new reality leads him into his destiny. The story of *The Matrix* is, in many ways, an allegory of the world we live in today. The really scary thought is that you're connected to the "grid," performing a function that doesn't utilize your gifts and talents. You're simply doing what you've been programmed to do. But you know it's not who you really are. Like Neo, you have to bust out. Instinctively, you know the pathway to your destiny, your purpose, lies beyond your ability to see from where you are right now. It's going to take considerable faith and courage to disconnect from the "grid" and follow your recurring dream.

Another favorite movie scene of mine is from *Joe Versus the Volcano*, starring Tom Hanks. Joe has a terrible job and a despicable boss. He's become a hypochondriac, anesthetized to the whole meaning of life, and feels he's lost his soul. He quits his job and takes off on a wild adventure where he meets up with Patricia (played by Meg Ryan). The two are having a discussion about life and beliefs when she says to Joe: *"My father says that almost the whole world is asleep. Everybody you know. Everybody you see. Everybody you talk to. He says that only a few people are awake, and they live in a state of constant total amazement."*

Like those zombies in the old horror movie, *Night of the Living Dead*, he's saying that most people are just moving around but not really alive. People who "sleepwalk" through life are lethargic and have no goals because they've allowed their dreams to be pushed down by others and forgotten. They're performing functions that have no productive purpose. There's activity but no reason for it. You must become one of the "wide-awake" people full of wonder, allowing yourself to be amazed at the scope and grandeur of life and the fact that you get to be a part of it all. You have an integral part to play in life's grand drama. Stay awake. Look for clues. Don't miss your cues.

The idea of change makes most people squirm. You'll feel this resistance when you start telling others about your dreams. It's human nature to process everything through the filter of how your dream and the resulting change might affect them. Since your dream is basically a complete unknown, the almost universal knee-jerk reaction is going to be negative from most people. Sociologists refer to this as the "herd instinct." It's simply a strong desire to keep things as they are and not upset the status quo.

There's a comical word picture in the Bible that advises, "Don't cast your pearls before swine." The "swine" in the story are the negative people who have no vision and don't want anybody else to have one either. They're dream stealers. Your recurring dream or vision provides you with valuable clues about the direction you should be heading. It's important here that you understand that I'm not talking about the common definition of dreams where you go to bed, go to sleep, and have a dream. No, what I mean when I use the term *dream* or *vision* has more to do with what preoccupies your thoughts during your waking hours. In other words, what's holding your attention? What keeps resonating with you? That's a clue! Your dream is the fire that energizes you toward your destiny. Don't allow dream stealers to extinguish it. And, by the way, don't allow your own negative thinking to do it either.

Clue 2.—Gifts and Talents

What are you just naturally good at? You've always been good at it. It comes easy to you. I'm amazed at how a real mechanic can open the hood of a car, poke around for two minutes, and pinpoint the problem. Sometimes he can just listen and know what's going on inside an engine. If you're mechanically minded, you know exactly what I'm talking about and that's a clue! If you're an artistic individual, however, you're probably not going to be fulfilled working in a garage.

Some people have the uncanny ability to think abstractly, which makes them remarkable problem solvers or creative geniuses. We find people like this in "think tanks," creating complex strategies or delving deeply into solving dilemmas that have eluded others. They are able to unravel tangled messes. Or they might be computer programmers involved in creating complex programs for video games, or writers creating screenplays for television and movies. Still others have a great ability to encourage and motivate people to achieve goals they could never accomplish on their own. These individuals are often coaches or leaders in sales organizations. It's not uncommon for people to overlook their unique gifts and talents simply because they don't see them as any big deal. Talk to your *"Who."* They may have a perspective of your gifts and talents that you're unable to see. What you're good at and what you enjoy are major clues to connecting with your destiny. Don't minimize their importance.

Clue 3.—Birds of a Feather

This is not complicated, so don't make it so. When you're on the right track, moving in the right direction, there will be a resonance with others moving along in the same stream. You're on parallel courses. There's an unspoken acceptance. You're all moving in the same direction. None of you are there yet, your final destinations may be different, but for now you're all on your way. You'll sense a nod of recognition from others letting you know they think you belong. It's like great musicians meeting to play together for the first time. It just doesn't take long for Eric Clapton and B. B. King to get in sync. When you're in the groove, doing what you're supposed to be doing, with the people you're supposed to be doing it with, everything "clicks." You're on the same wavelength. It's a sense of not only finding yourself but also of discovering there are others swimming alongside you in this stream. The initial fear or anxiety rush you may have felt when you first entered this stream begins to dissipate as you realize you're not alone. You have friends here who hold different positions. Some are on your same level and are your fellow seekers. Others are here for you to help. Still others are in higher positions and can open doors for you. The important thing to remember about streams is that you need to find one where you intuitively feel a sense of belonging. It's almost tribal. All of a sudden you have access and favor that you haven't had in other streams with other people. You have friends and friends of friends who will help you simply because they feel you're part of them, they are part of you, and you like each other. There exists a natural preference. Pay attention. Stay alert. If you have found your "stream," if you have been accepted by a "tribe"—don't take this for granted. It's another important clue.

CLUE 4.—REJECTION

Everybody hates this one. After all, what kind of an idiot wouldn't recognize your worth, your wonderful wit and charm, your talent, skills, good looks, and keen intellect? To know you is to love you, right? Wrong. More than 800,000

Tutsi were slaughtered by the Hutu tribe in Africa simply because they looked down on them. There are people who will cut your head off (figuratively speaking) for no other reason than you're swimming in their stream and they think you don't belong. You're not wearing the right gang colors. There's not a thing in the world you can do about it, so don't even try. It wouldn't matter if you rode in on a giant pig, bare naked, with your hair on fire. They're just not going to be impressed with anything you do. You can't win because they won't let you win. They don't like you. You're not one of them. You're an outsider, an interloper, not of their tribe. These are not your people. You can bust your butt trying to win them over, but you never will. You're a square peg, they're round holes. If you try to reshape yourself in order to fit in, you will only make yourself more miserable.

There were two minutes left in the basketball game when the coach finally called my name. "Beaudine," he shouted almost reluctantly, "I guess you can go in now." My team was losing, 50–32, so I really had no reason to be all that excited. Still, I had this crazy feeling that if I could just do a couple of things well, the coach would see me in a more positive light and might give me a shot at playing more than just when the game was out of reach.

My dad, standing high in the corner of the stands, pumped his arm in excitement as I went to the scorer's table to enter the game. I felt bad for him. He had been so loyal to attend all my games, hoping to watch me play but usually all he got to see was me warming the bench. I glanced up at him with gratitude, but when my coach saw my brief acknowledgment, he angrily hissed, "Get your head in the game, Beaudine, you horse's ass!" "Thanks, Coach," I thought to myself as the game resumed.

I took the inbounds pass down the court and found myself alone at the top of the key. I took the shot and "swish!" Nothin' but net on my first try! Wow! Now that felt good! The opposing team's inbounds play was thwarted as our other guard stole the ball and hit me on a great pass for an easy layup. The pace quickened at the other end of the court when their shot missed and I managed to pull down the rebound. Taking off down the court at full sprint, I hit my teammate with a solid pass, and he went in for the layup. Wanting to impress the coach, he was a little too anxious and missed the shot. Fortunately, I was coming up fast from behind and grabbed the easy rebound and made the layup. Now, I'm really pumped! I've been in the game for only thirty-two seconds and I've scored 6 points—the most points I had gotten the whole year combined! The opposing team drove down but missed its shot. We drove back, passing the ball around three or four times when, all of a sudden, I was left open in the corner, so I took a shot from fifteen feet out, and, to my astonishment, "swish," it went in! The adrenaline was really pumping now, and the whole team could feel the momentum of the game shifting in our favor. Amazingly, we stole the ball again, and once again I just happened to be in the right place at the right time. Running flat out, I took the pass and, with a quick stop, turned and jumped up near the basket. The easy bank shot went in for my tenth point in under a minute! I couldn't believe this was happening! The crowd of eighteen or so was going nuts; the score was now 50–42! Just then, when everything was going great, my coach called for a time-out. As I started to walk off the court, I heard him yell, "Beaudine—you hog! Get off the court. First team, you're in!" I was stunned, embarrassed, and confused. I had outscored everybody on my team so far and created fresh hope and excitement. But now the crowd went quiet; the momentum died. We lost, 50–42.

Watch out for the "hog callers." You've probably had a similar experience at some point in your life. You were doing something great, making a real contribution and feeling pretty good about it when, all of a sudden, you got "called down." Not only were you not appreciated, you were reprimanded and even punished for performing well. I'd venture to say that's also about the time you began to realize life often isn't fair. It happens a lot. You speak up at the meeting and someone laughs or squelches your great idea. You tell people about a new product/technique/song lyric, and someone submarines your idea as stupid or unrealistic. You tell someone confidentially about your dreams and goals, and they become threatened by your confidence and possible success and begin to sabotage you by telling you (and sometimes those around you) that your idea is a pipe dream. Ouch. Even worse, the "hog caller" could even be a family member. Double Ouch!

When my "hog-calling" coach ambushed me with his well aimed "put-down," I wanted to run and hide. I not only wanted to quit the team, I also felt like I never wanted to play basketball ever again. Fortunately, I did play again. I didn't allow that "hog caller" to kill my love for the game or my desire to play.

Listen, my friend, there are "dream killers" and "hog callers" everywhere. Some are loud and "in your face," like my coach. Others can be very subtle and much quieter, but their intention, whether conscious or unconscious, is still the same. "Hog callers" put you down, keep you from performing at your best, and kill your spirit. They don't wish you well, but instead desire to control you within their limited parameters designed to "keep you in your place." Whenever you allow someone else to design your life for you, they'll always design it way too small. If your boss, coach, teacher, regional vice president, whatever is a "hog caller," you need to recognize what's going on. My dad called this "getting a clue." A clue is a hint that maybe you're on the wrong team, you're hanging with the wrong crowd, or you're working for the wrong company.

Rejection is a severe teacher and you'll most likely log some time in this classroom at some point in your life. But rejection can be even more instructive than favor because it forces you to come to grips with who you really are and who you're not. It lets you know where you don't belong and who you don't belong with. The sooner you get out of there and locate the right stream, the better off you're going to be. A lot of people try two or three streams, get rejected, and give up. They begin to think they don't belong in any stream, so they stop trying. Big Mistake! There's a stream for you. There's a flow that fits you. You have friends who will lead you to it and help you in. So keep looking for your *"Who!"*

"You hog!" I'll never forget those words. They motivated me. They still do. They showed me that success is geographical. Here's what that means:

> **!** Go where you're celebrated,
> **■** not just tolerated.

Your pot of gold (whatever that represents to you) won't be found with people who don't like you. You'll never succeed with people who devalue you. They have no appreciation for your gifts and talents or the contribution you bring. Your real pot of gold is with your *"Who."* These are your friends who love you, want to see you succeed, and enjoy sharing your dreams. You can count on them. So, from one "hog" to another, keep your dream alive!

CLUE 5.—DO WHAT YOU LOVE

Kahlil Gibran, the beloved author, said it best in his classic book, *The Prophet*: *"And think not that you can direct the course of Love, for Love, if it finds you worthy, directs your course."*

Doing what you "love" is one of the most essential components of finding your dream. One of the great disconnects of life, a truly monumental error that people commonly make, is not allowing love to direct their course. Why? Because they don't know their own hearts, so they distrust themselves and their natural instincts. Just think what would happen to the lion out on the plains if he didn't trust his own instincts. He would starve. When you allow yourself to be so programmed by the culture you're in that you become disconnected from your own heart, you're in major trouble. You render yourself unable to make decisions about what is best for your life and the lives of those you love. The real danger here is that you will begin to follow somebody else's idea of success and fulfillment. What if the lion in Africa forgot he was a lion and began to think of himself as a water buffalo? We would say that's a ridiculous, foolish way for a lion to try to live. Doesn't he know he's a lion? This is exactly what multitudes of people do every day. They forget *"Who"* and *"What"* they are. They attempt to become someone or something else for which they're ill suited, and there are several possible reasons for this.

■ **They Want to Be Somebody Else** A person may admire someone for their achievements in life and want to be like them. But they don't possess that person's level of talent, skill, or charisma. Unfortunately, a lot of people live in their own fantasy world, falsely believing they do have what it takes. This is a Big Mistake and a huge time waster.

■ **They Need the Money** This will turn a lion into a water buffalo quicker than anything else. I believe that working to pay the bills is one of the most common causes in forgetting your dream. So many people are just too tired at the end of the day to work on or even think about their dream. Too bad. Turn off the damn TV! The TV will suck your dream right into the black hole of oblivion. Refuse to veg—unless, of course, your dream is to become a vegetable.

■ **Somebody Else Told Them What to Do** They allowed a parent, teacher, preacher, or some other authority figure to manufacture what they thought was a good identity for them. All of us need wise counselors and good guidance, but only from those who have no other agenda except to help us discover and develop what we love and are well suited for. Allowing someone else to remake you into their image will rob you of personal satisfaction, peace of mind, and contentment. Don't allow anyone to derail you from your destiny.

The number one reason so many people haven't allowed love to direct their path is because they really don't believe they can do what they love, with the people they love, in a place they love, and be happy, successful, and fulfilled.

What you love is a "major clue." For example, if you love art, well, guess what? That's a huge industry that covers the globe. Which kinds of art do you love—music, painting, literature? Music is just one branch of the art world, and there are myriads of styles. Begin asking yourself where you might fit in.

Every organization will welcome the passionate worker with the right skill set and great attitude. The only way you can have passion is to be inspired by something you love. So ask yourself, "What do I love?" You may not know yet exactly what you want to do. You may need some more knowledge about the industry that interests you before you can see where you might fit. But once you determine what you love, you'll have the clue you need to push you further along on the path toward connecting with your dream. Begin to look around the landscape of your life for people who love what you love. Begin to talk to them. You may be surprised to discover you already know someone who can open a door for you—someone who likes you enough to act as a bridge for you.

A BRAND-NEW DREAM

I was in my midtwenties when I first joined my dad's executive search firm, Eastman & Beaudine. I accepted the company's goals for me as I worked on the searches they assigned me
in manufacturing, engineering, and technology. I never really
thought about this being *the* job; I was just seeking a field
where I felt I could excel and where I liked the people I worked
with and they liked me. I became very successful. But after
several years of doing the same thing, I began to develop a
growing uneasiness and a longing for something more. I liked
executive search, but I loved sports. I'd often wonder if there
could be any way I could involve my passion for sports with
my career as an executive recruiter.

One day I approached my dad and expressed the frustra-
tion I was feeling. He asked me two very simple yet direct
questions, "What do you want to do? What do you love?"

All of a sudden the thoughts and feelings I had been experiencing came rushing together and crystallized in my mind. I
felt like the kid in the movie *A Christmas Story* who wanted a
particular BB gun as a present. When the department store
Santa asked him what he wanted for Christmas, he momen-
tarily froze. He couldn't get the words out. But then, all of a
sudden, they came flowing like a torrent. He blurted out an
exact description of the object of his desire. Standing in his office that day, my dad was asking me basically the same question, and, for a moment, I froze like a deer caught in headlights.
But then in a flash, I began to speak with clarity, "There is a
burgeoning sports and entertainment industry out there that
we're missing. They need executives, too. I'd like to develop a
division in our firm that would accommodate these fields.
When I place an executive as president of a manufacturing
company, at the end of my search, I get a tour of the plant. But

if I place the head of marketing for a professional sports league, I get great tickets for All-Star Weekend! From now on I want a majority of my search work to be in the fields of sports and entertainment!" There, I said it! Alarms were set off! I heard bells ringing! It was a great epiphany! Surprisingly, my dad responded to my youthful enthusiasm by saying, "Great. Go get it!" Stunned and speechless, I asked, "Go get what?"

"Go get the NBA and all the other sports and entertainment searches you want!" he answered. "Your dream is closer than you think, Bob."

I floated out of his office almost in a dream state. The gates of heaven had been flung wide open! I could now match my passion for sports and entertainment with a business I was good at—executive search.

But there was one caveat. I'd still be required to do my regular job. I still had to bring in money and fill searches in the industries that were the financial foundation of our firm. I saw that as a good thing. I enjoyed my associations with the people I worked with, and I was good at it. I'd need to stay sharp while developing this new dream. Besides, most of the people I worked with loved sports and entertainment as much as I did.

If you're going after your dreams and goals, you're going to have to do some things you've never done. How badly do you want it? Are you willing to do what you've never done to have what you've never had?

You might have a lot of thoughts and ideas swimming around in your head but you can't quite sort it all out yet. Very often it takes an outside agent, someone who will listen, to act as the catalyst to help you collect your random thoughts into a cohesive whole.

■ Sometimes it just takes a simple question, like the one my dad asked me, to begin the flow that brings all those tributaries of thought into a common stream.

■ Sometimes, it takes someone who sees something in you that you can't see in yourself and is able to speak it to you in a way that enables you to see it, too.

■ Sometimes someone gives you permission to do what you've always wanted to do.

DALE CARNEGIE, MARY, AND ME

I was once forced to take the Dale Carnegie course. I was working for the Carnation Company, and management thought of me as one of their rising young stars. But my ego was larger than my character, and I could be a little brash with people. Like a lot of young, talented people, I was oblivious to the effect I was having on others around me. I had just been promoted from the sales office in Dallas to the marketing department at the headquarters in Los Angeles. I was having difficulty getting along with some specific sales managers (who I thought needed the course more than me). However, my superiors thought the course would help me be a better supervisor and basically ordered me to sign up.

The Dale Carnegie course lasted for twelve weeks and was all about teaching you how to strengthen your interpersonal relationships, better handle stress, and adapt to a fast-changing workplace. It used team dynamics, and the teachers/facilitators were superb. What's amazing is you never hear a negative word in the class. You give a couple of speeches a night; you read several books, including the classic *How to Win Friends and Influence People*. Most of the thirty or so people in my class seemed to want to get better at public speaking and soften the edges of their personality. Initially, I thought the course was a joke—until I heard Mary's story. She was an orphan whose husband had recently left her for another woman. Her accounting firm had transferred her from Sacramento to L.A. She told us she hadn't yet made any new friends since the move. She appeared shy, sad, and hurt, which were all major hindrances to being a good public speaker. During the third week of the class, we were each required to give an impromptu speech. Our teacher would give an arbitrary subject as the common topic. That night's topic was to be on pets. This was Mary's chance to improve on her earlier performances where she'd completely bombed. All of a sudden she became animated. Mary was passionate, energized, and joyful as she talked about her boxer, Lucille. Afterward, the teacher asked me to share three positive things I had received from Mary's talk. I was to address my remarks directly to Mary. I began by telling her, "Great job, Mary! You really know a lot about dogs and pets in general. Tonight you were relaxed and confident as you gave your speech. You clearly had everyone's attention. I have to tell you, Mary, if I were you, I wouldn't be an accountant any longer. You've convinced me, and I think everyone in the room, that you should be a veterinarian. I'm sure I'm not the first to say this to you, but I believe this is your calling."

Mary seemed different after that night. Everyone's perception of her was elevated. She was becoming more confident, and each week she became more and more vocal at encouraging others in the class. The night of Mary's speech was a turning point for all of us. The rest of the course sailed.

On graduation night all the members of the class were asked to tell a story about what affected them most during the last twelve weeks. When it was Mary's turn to address the class, she stood up and said: "When I began this course I was a shy, unhappy divorcée with no friends, family, or hope. Today, I stand here a changed woman. My happiness is that I found each and every one of you! This class, this community of friends, has touched my soul in ways you can't imagine. I hope you all don't feel uncomfortable when I tell you that you saved my life! I have written each of you a personal letter, but I'd like to read the one I wrote to Bob Beaudine."

I was shocked when she spoke my name.

> Dear Bob, she continued, thank you. How did you know that I hated my job in accounting? That deep down I had a secret dream of always wanting to be a veterinarian? I have dreamed about it since I was nine years old. But no one ever encouraged me to follow my dream until you spoke to me about it that night just a few weeks ago. I have to tell you, my heart leaped when you said that it was my "calling." And you said it with such authority and conviction that for the first time in my life I was convinced I could do this. Well, I'm pleased to report to all of you tonight that I start my new job as a veterinarian's assistant at the animal hospital next week. They are allowing me to go back to school part-time so I can follow my dream of becoming a veterinarian. Bob, it was your encouragement that placed me there. So tonight I want to give you the same gift you gave me. I want to tell you something about yourself, Bob. I want to encourage you as you encouraged me. I have listened and watched you now for twelve weeks, and I have to tell you: just as I'm no accountant; you're no product manager. You should be in job placement, maybe even a recruiter! And even better, Bob, if I may be so bold, it's very easy for me to see you one day as a motivational speaker. I believe that's your calling!

I just smiled and thanked her for her encouragement but was unconvinced. However, the passage of time has proven Mary right. Two years later I was in executive recruiting, where I have remained for twenty-nine years. And motivational speaking has become my passion. How could she have seen that so long ago? How did she know? The answer is surprisingly simple. When we allow others access to our personal world, we give them the opportunity to see into us in ways we're not able to see ourselves. Help others see the potential you see in them and allow others to give you clues about what they see in you. Everyone involved will enjoy the view.

REWORKING YOU AND YOUR *"WHO"*

What Used to Work Doesn't Work Anymore.
—FRANK BEAUDINE

Forget balance; it's just a fantasy that authors like to write about because it sounds good. But it's really a lot of nonsense, because it's impossible to achieve. There's a whole lot of people out there driving themselves crazy trying to "live a balanced life."

There was a guy on TV years ago who did an amazing routine spinning plates. He would put a plate on a stick and give it a spin. He would continue the same process until he had about a dozen plates spinning all at one time. Now, that's balance! But how long was he able to sustain that? Not long. The man would frantically run up and down the length of the table in an effort to keep those plates spinning. My point is, even if you could get your life in balance, how long do you think you could keep it there? My guess would be about three seconds, which is close to the same length of time the planets stay lined up when they converge.

Elizabeth was a management consultant for one of the top

firms in the country. We were sitting next to each other on a plane from New York to Dallas. We hit it off immediately and talked most of the flight home. She was smart and attractive with a dynamic personality. It was obvious she enjoyed the rapid pace and challenge of her job. She could articulate what success looked like at any point in relation to her client assignments. Elizabeth knew all the strategic imperatives of success. When it came to goals, means, message, and tactics, she had it down. She knew exactly what to do and had the discipline to execute her strategy. But, when our discussion turned to her personal life, her entire demeanor changed. Her Harvard MBA and strategic imperatives were not instructive when it came to her interpersonal relationships.

Her keen intellect that, only moments earlier, was clearly articulating her professional life dulled as her speech trailed off into a quiet mumble about her personal life not working all that well. She told me she had focused too much on the *"What"* in life instead of the *"Who."* Since moving to Dallas and recently having a child, she and her husband hadn't made any new friends outside work. Their marriage relationship had waned considerably due to the demands of the new baby coupled with their work schedules. It had been quite a while since she had considered her personal goals and dreams. In fact, she had forgotten most of them entirely.

REWORKING YOU

When you come to the realization that what used to work beautifully in your life is no longer working, it's time to take a fresh look at the "Seven Components Involved in Reinventing Your Life."

The first three focus on *"You,"* the last four on your *"Who."*

1. *Reevaluate Your Circumstances*

Elizabeth's dilemma is not all that uncommon. Like so many of her peers, she's so busy pouring her energy into her professional endeavors that by the time she gets home she's drained, done for the day. In addition, her own health, happiness, and long-term desires and dreams keep getting pushed into the back of her mind. She is starting to forget.

A lifestyle that was once healthy, vibrant, and beneficial can turn toxic when our life circumstances change significantly. Attempting to superimpose an old agenda onto a whole new set of circumstances doesn't work. In the same way, a single person who marries must make lifestyle changes to accommodate the marriage; we must make the changes that will ensure the best chance of success in our new situation. But in order to do that, we need to hit the "pause" button in life just long enough to reevaluate and make the needed course corrections.

In Elizabeth's case, there had been a profound change in her circumstances—namely, the new baby. She was not prepared for the impact this was having on her career and marriage. She and her husband needed some time away with the baby as a family. They would benefit greatly by taking a few days to reflect and talk about all the changes in their lives. Some time away from all their distractions would allow them to reevaluate their priorities. A proper reevaluation of their current reality would reveal that Elizabeth and her husband needed an environment that would promote the happiness and well-being of the whole family. Unfortunately, most people don't take the time to regularly reevaluate their lives. They continue to plow ahead with the unconscious and incorrect belief that "things will somehow work out." Big Mistake!

This is where the joy of living begins to get numbed. Where our dreams go into a dormant stage and forgetfulness begins to creep in. When the dream finally does resurface, it seems further away and almost impossible to achieve. This is the place where we start accepting second best. Far too many people live the rest of their lives right here. It's been said that the hardest position to play in an orchestra is second fiddle. Settling for second best is hard in any area of life.

2. *Reassess Your Influences*

I can change your world by evaluating just *three* things: what you read, what you listen to, and *"Who"* your friends are.

■ *What You Read*

I made a huge mistake earlier in my life by not reading more. Whatever your age, I want to encourage you to read, read, and read as much as you can! I once heard Jim Rohn (one of the top motivational speakers in the country) say:

> Everything you need for your better future and success has already been written. And guess what? It's all available. All you have to do is go to the library. But would you believe that only three percent of the people in America have a library card? Wow, they must be expensive! No, they're free. And there's probably a library in every neighborhood."

I'm now the proud owner of a library card. Do yourself an enormous favor. Join the ranks of the three percent today! It's probably not a coincidence that three percent of the country possesses 97 percent of the wealth. All the success books I've read agree with Jim.

> **{ ! }** "There is no difference between someone who can't read and one who chooses not to read. They both end up the same—ignorant."

This past year I decided to do some continuing education by reading fifty-two books—one per week. You might think that's excessive, but it was one of the best things I've ever done. It was an amazing and fun experience to have the ideas of so many fascinating and successful authors going through my head. But I didn't always feel that way. I would pass by the "how to be a success" area at major bookstores and purposely not pick up anything because I thought the authors were just trying to get rich by snookering me into buying their books. What I discovered during my reading campaign is that most of these success writers were already rich and didn't need my money. I began to understand they had something of tremendous value to impart. They had achieved success in their field, and the thought of sharing their knowledge to help others was something they found exciting and meaningful. Their primary motivation was to help others succeed. They enjoyed explaining strategies that work to those who are wise enough to stop and listen.

One of the fifty-two books I read had a statistic from the National Sales Association that really caught my eye. It said it usually takes five sales calls to earn someone's business. Not just five e-mails or telephone calls, but five "personal meetings" to build a relationship. The book went on to say, however, that 50 percent of sales reps quit after the first call if they didn't land the business right on the spot, 30 percent quit after the third call, and 10 percent more quit after the fourth try. Amazingly, only 10 percent of salespeople had the persistence to call on a potential client all five times in order to land the business!

This statistic bothered me so much that I immediately reviewed my calls for the last two years and, to my astonishment, discovered I had actually called on two companies four times and given up! I couldn't believe it. Like the ones I had just read about, I had quit too. Once I saw it, I got on a plane and flew out to meet each of them. I explained I had read a book this year saying it takes five calls to earn someone's business, and that I was here for my fifth call! They laughed! One of the two clients remarked, "Is that your sales pitch?" I jokingly said, "Yes, and I'm sticking with it!" To my surprise, both clients told me it was good timing because they needed my services. I got the business from both companies! Needless to say, I was stunned! Let's do a quick recap: I read a book that cost me $29 and plucked out one great idea that earned me $225,000! I told myself I need to read more!

■ *What You Listen To*

There is a big difference between hearing and listening. Hearing can be almost an unconscious awareness of sounds. Many people who live under an airport flight path develop the ability to "tune out" the sound of jet engines. Listening, however, is something more. Listening is active hearing. It's intentional. You're involved. You are "tuned in" to what you are hearing. When you listen you learn.

If you spend a portion of your time each day in a car, on a train, a treadmill, a bike, walking or taking a long lunch, you can greatly enhance your learning. Consider using that time intentionally to develop a skill that would help you get closer to your dream.

I have several *"Who"* friends in California and New York who drive at least an hour to and from work each day. But two hours of "alone time" each day adds up to almost 500 hours of learning and growing a year. When you utilize (make use of) your travel time to listen and learn, you'll enhance every other area in your life.

■ *"Who"* Your Friends Are

Now would be a great time to reevaluate your associations and make some decisions about whom you're going to walk with into the future. Personal and professional relationships can be intricate and sometimes hard to figure out. But, according to author Bill Hybels, there are three general categories that offer a good starting place to evaluate the residual effect that each relational encounter has on you. They are draining, neutral, and replenishing.

■ **Draining** This one is the most obvious. We all have at least one. These people just wear you out. You groan at the thought of seeing them. When they come into the room, life starts to go out of you like air from a leaky balloon. And if they start talking . . . you may as well stick a pin in the balloon. The lingering effect this person seems to have on you is one of depleted energy. It just takes something out of you every time you deal with such people.

■ **Neutral** These are folks who really don't affect your emotional thermostat very much, if at all. You don't have any personal expectations of them other than the function they perform. They could be some people you work with but not closely. You see them every day. You like them, they like you, but that's about it. You might even be on a first-name basis but there's no meaningful interaction required or needed. We all have these people in our lives every day and we're necessary to each another. But the relationship is simply on a functional level. This is not meant to diminish anyone's value. You simply can't be friends with everybody and everybody can't be friends with you.

■ **Replenishing** Ahhh—These are your life givers. Generally speaking, there are just some people in the world who make it a better place. You're always glad to see them. Mainly because they seem to be genuinely glad to see you. They bring relief and seem to brighten every room they walk into. On a more personal level, this could be your spouse or a close friend whom you love. Their presence is refreshing and stimulating. A moment ago you were in the doldrums, tense, brooding over some problem or issue. This person shows up and says two words and your whole environment is transformed into a pretty nice place. They bring out the best in you. Inwardly, your heart opens and moves toward your replenishers.

We've all heard people say something like, "Oh, I've got lots of friends!" No they don't. Not really. Such a person has no concept that real friendship requires intimacy, depth and commitment. You can't have "lots of friends" because no one has the time or emotional space to be close friends with more than just a few. The "Inner Circle" is the smallest circle but it's also the most powerful. There may be many people in and around your life but each one of the relationships will be on a different level. It is a wise person who discerns and understands how each one functions and contributes to the overall environment.

Imagine for a moment you were one of the 16 people in that garage with Bill Gates creating Microsoft. Have you ever seen the picture of them all together? It's a classic. They looked like skater dudes, smoking pot and drinking Rolling Rock. I guarantee you none of them could have ever dreamed that many of them would become billionaires simply because of *"Who"* they were hanging out with. Like most start-ups, Microsoft certainly had its share of people who were "just along for the ride," but at least they were savvy enough to sense something extraordinary was happening. They saw something in Bill Gates and Paul Allen that wasn't just good, but great!

People with great ideas enjoy sharing them, but people with only good ideas typically aren't as generous. They actually seem worried that you might take their one good idea!

Consequently, I strongly urge you to continually reevaluate your associations. All it takes is one great mentor, coach, or friend to share the insight that will help you leapfrog over your competition or help get you back on track. But this will only happen if you're humble and wise enough to stop, listen, and take some notes.

3. *Tell Yourself the Truth*

There may be an unfamiliar path you will need to walk to get going in the direction of your dream or a goal. There might be a few pitfalls and unexpected twists and turns along the way. Do yourself a favor—put a proper spin on things. You don't need to put on rose-colored glasses; just take off the dark ones.

Be aware of what you're telling yourself and don't talk yourself into defeat. Instead, begin to speak in an affirming way to yourself. There are thoughts going on up there in your head. The truly wonderful and amazing fact is that you have the incredible power to decide what thoughts you will think. Here is a very valuable insight:

> **[!]** Most people listen to themselves instead of talk to themselves.

When self-defeating thoughts slither their way into your mind, and they will try, don't let them go unchallenged! You don't have to put up with it. It may sound a little crazy but the quickest way to transform your thoughts (and your mood) is to start speaking out loud to yourself. Speak words that are life-affirming, truthful and joyful. You'll be amazed how well it works. So, when you find your thoughts wandering around in the dark trying to get you afraid and depressed, turn on the light! See yourself succeeding and enjoying living your dream.

You're never too late or too early or too young or too old or too anything to accomplish that special purpose or land that cool job or rediscover that lost dream and get it back on track. Tiger Woods, Michelle Wie, and LeBron James don't feel they are too young to beat you! The American public didn't think President Reagan was too old to lead the country. There's a wise old saying about the value of persistence:

> **{!}** We don't play nine-inning games in life; we play to the end!

I love that quote, because it clearly communicates a message of genuine hope, a truthful message that says, "Hey, it ain't over till it's over!" Sometimes miracles hide. There could be something just around the corner that you can't see yet that will open up a whole, new exciting world to you.

Reworking Your "Who"

Okay, we've just covered the first *three* of the "Seven Components of Reinventing Your Life." They're all about you . . . Now let's dive into the last *four*, which are all about your *"Who."*

4. *Cultivate Your* "Who"

There are leaders in every field of life who are so good at what they do that others recognize it and embrace the leader's philosophy.

I have a friend in Mexico who sells time-shares. Through my association with him I learned that only the top 3 percent of time-share sales reps operate according to the "100/40 Strategy." Their primary goal during the first few years in the business is to build a base of a hundred clients. It takes hard work and long hours, but in the long run, it pays off big time! These one hundred clients get the royal treatment from the rep. They are nurtured, cultivated, and pampered with great customer service. It's a matter of perspective. The top 3 percent sales reps actually see their one hundred clients very differently than the other 97 percent do. They don't compartmentalize them into a sector called business, but instead see their clients as friends. They spend a lot of time thanking their "Special 100" and are always on the alert for whatever they can do extra for them. Their three-word mantra is "Yes, I can!" They help them with hotel arrangements, cars, restaurants, babysitters, and a better location on the property—whatever. They help with weddings, birthday parties, and anniversaries—nothing is too much to ask. They think of their "Special 100" as gifts in their lives, and it shows.

Why would these sales reps do all this work instead of making more calls and getting more sales revenue for the company? Because they understand that by taking extra care of these "Special 100" clients, they're securing the key to their present and future success. "Special 100" clients, shown extra care and attention, will be their golden egg, their oil well, or their IPO (initial public offering) over the coming years. What these top 3 percent have learned is that if you focus single-mindedly on your "Special 100" they will:

■ Buy one more week on the property;

■ Upgrade from a one bedroom to a two or three bedroom;

■ Introduce you to their best friends who will also buy a time-share;

■ Tell your boss you're the greatest and the top reason they are there!

What does this all mean? It means more sales and happier customers and a more enjoyable lifestyle! Wouldn't life be a little better if we were surrounded and assisted by people who loved and cared for us?

The top 3 percent time-share sales reps *see* it! What do the other 97 percent do? After their first one hundred they spend all their time and energy going after their *next* one hundred. It's like shutting down the oil rig after harvesting only one hundred barrels then racing off to dig another well, even though there's a lot more oil down there in the first one! But the top 3 percent time-share reps don't make that mistake. They treasure what they've been given and also expect to meet new people that they "click" with from time to time. When they do, they don't let them get away, because they know a rare gem when they see it. My friend in Mexico who sells time-shares became so successful with this strategy that he was rewarded with a raise and made sales manager so he could train the other salespeople in the art of "friendship selling." Now he gets a commission from every sale made on the property.

So how do you cultivate your *"Who?"* This is the fun part. And it's simple. You call a friend on the phone and invite them out for breakfast or lunch or whatever. Get tickets to a ball game and include your friend. You just start getting reinvolved in the lives of your *"Who."* Take the initiative, make the call. You'll be glad you did.

5. *Multiply Your* "Who"

The best sales reps intentionally help and assist in any way they can. They understand the principle of sowing and reaping. If you sow genuine care and attentive service into your clients' lives, you will continually reap a bountiful harvest. Here's the way it works: if your "100 List" of special friends are telling their "100 List" that you're great, guess what? You're automatically great in the eyes of at least 10,000 people! If you're a time-share rep and your "Special 100" are telling their "Special 100" that your property is great, then those friends believe it. When those friends decide to look at a time-share property, guess who they call? The other 97 percent of sales reps don't get it because they can't see past their noses. They're looking only for a short-term gain. They tend to see people as "marks" instead of potential long-term friends. These people don't understand the power and value of true friendship, so they fail to keep the connection to their first "100." They are forever running around looking for a new well to dig. Big Mistake!

When I first got into the executive recruiting business, my dad gave me some great advice. "Bob," he said, "sales is always about making friends first, because your friends will do business with you." Too many people are always seeking something else and missing something more! The top time-share reps, however, don't make that mistake. They do something the others don't—they focus on their "100!"

When we begin to recognize the Power of *"WHO!"* and the great things we can do through our *"Who,"* we'll start to see how our dreams and goals can become reality.

6. *Concentric Circles*

The paradigm people have for getting things done is all messed up today. They are focusing way too much effort on the *"What"* in life and not the *"Who."* Best-selling author and internationally recognized leadership expert John Maxwell wrote in his book, *Talent Is Never Enough:* "As long as there are people in the world, there will be plenty of talent. If that were enough, everyone would reach their potential. What's missing are things people need in addition to their talent."

What you need is your *"Who."* Friends can help you move your dreams and goals into the real world. We all have concentric circles of close friends, and they touch each other in amazing ways. Your *"Who"* helps my *"Who,"* and my *"Who"* can help yours. This is where life gets good. We should always be thinking about our *"Who"*!

■ "Who" *Helps Even Strangers*

I have a close friend named Tom Dooley who hosts one of the top radio shows in the country, *The Journey*. He has this deep, soothing voice that he uses to narrate and comment from books while playing soft music underneath. After about three or four minutes, he will play a song that relates to his subject matter. All of Tom's material is very encouraging and is wildly popular, especially among baby boom listeners looking for some real inspiration. He receives letters every day from people all over the country who tell how their lives were changed by something poignant he said on the air. He doesn't always remember what he said, but they do! Tom has that rare quality of making you think he is speaking directly to you.

For example, he called me one day and told me the tragic story of a couple he heard about from some close friends. Their son was a soldier serving in Iraq and was returning home after spending a very intense year on the front lines. On the day he was to leave, he was ordered to spend one more day guarding what was supposed to be a safe area. But it wasn't safe and he was killed.

Several months before their son's death, the parents had planned an Alaskan cruise for their wedding anniversary. But now they decided not to go. However, close friends encouraged them to take the cruise believing it would be a time of much needed rest and healing. Tom called me because he knew our firm had placed the president of the cruise line in his position. He asked if there was anything that could be done to make the couple's vacation more memorable. I called my friend Jack, the president of the cruise line. He is one of the most giving people I know, and I knew that he would be touched by this story. He was, and things were put into motion to make special accommodations for the couple.

Follow the process:

■ One call by a special friend of the family to Tom Dooley asking for help for this couple in crisis.

■ One call from Tom to me describing the tragedy and asking for assistance.

■ One call from me to Jack asking for whatever help he might be able to give.

Everything fell into place. The soldier's parents were given VIP treatment and were upgraded several levels to a suite for the cruise. Jack set up the parents to dine with the captain of the ship. The cruise line made sure they had a great escape and could celebrate their son's life and memory. Now what's amazing about all this is that I've never talked to or met that couple. Neither has Tom or Jack. We were all just so honored to have played even a tiny part in the lives of these parents of a fallen war hero. You see, Tom and Jack are part of my "100 List." When they call, they get immediate access and vice versa. I try to do anything I can for them just because they're part of my "Who."

■ Breaking the Lease with Your "Who"

I once rented an apartment in another city for a family member that required me to co-sign the lease. Unforeseen circumstances abruptly changed our situation, and we no longer needed the apartment. But now I had a rather large problem. I had signed a lease for a year. I called the manager of the complex to ask if we could cancel the contract. Her answer was an abrupt and emphatic no. She explained they were moving into a slow time of year and there would be no opportunity to rent the apartment to someone else. I would be held responsible for the entire year's rent. I thought it was unfair to just slam the door in my face, so now I was feeling a little defensive and slightly angry. What could I do? My first thought was crying and then suing, but that's not how I was brought up. Sometimes when life presents circumstances we deem unacceptable, we panic and stop reasoning effectively. This can cause a sort of "temporary blindness" that can keep us from seeing a solution that may be right in front of us. Life has a way of sometimes presenting problems you can't solve yourself. You're "a cup short," and you're going to need help from someone else. This can be especially tough for people who don't feel worthy to receive help from others. But turn that around for a moment. How would you respond if an old friend you hadn't heard from in years suddenly called with a problem that you could easily solve? You'd probably be glad to hear from them and happy to help. Most of us really do like helping others and will go out of our way to help those we really care about. This is where the "100/40 Strategy" comes into play. Remember . . . *"You already know everyone you need to know."* You Got *"Who"!*

I thought through my "100 List" and began to look for someone that could help me. As I reviewed my list, I saw the name of an old college roommate who worked in the apartment-building business. I had no idea if he could help or not, but I had nothing to lose by asking. I called Steve and told him my dilemma and the result I hoped to accomplish. (Telling someone your desired result is an important key to getting what you want.) I told him I wanted the apartment manager to tear up the lease and let us out without payment. He laughed! But when he finished chuckling he asked me to look at the lease and find the name of the corporation that owned the specific complex. I read him the name. To my surprise Steve informed me that a former fraternity brother of ours was a senior executive in the corporation that owned this particular apartment complex. One call from Steve to Jim, and I was out of the lease! That's the Power of *"WHO!"*

You might say, "Bob, you have more friends than me. You have better *'Who,'* and I don't think I have *'Who'* friends that can help me in such a big way." But that's not true. The wonderful thing about this strategy is that it works at every level of life.

Let's say you're the one who encountered the problem with the apartment lease. You look on your "100 List" and don't see anyone in that business, but you do notice a name of a friend that you had lunch with last week who mentioned something about commercial real estate. So, you call your friend and explain your dilemma. Your friend tells you he knows someone who installs all the carpet for all those apartments. As it turns out, the carpet guy is married to the secretary of the president of the corporation that owns the property. Your problem is presented to the president by the carpet guy's wife. The president instructs her to "take care of it." You get a phone call from a woman you've never met who tells you you're off the hook. Now, that's how the "100/40 Strategy" works! You see, the difference between successful people and the crowd is that successful people ask good questions—and the first question should always be *"Who"?*

7. *Investing in Your* "Who"

Do you know your *"Who"?* In my business, I've developed a database of over 5,365 people that can say, "Hi, Bob." That really doesn't mean a lot except that I know a lot of people because of my business. I had what I thought was a great networking strategy, but I was about to discover I was dead wrong. I used to try to touch 1,000 or so a year with notes and calls and visits. It was exhausting. I have over five million miles accumulated on American Airlines to show for it! One day I stopped and studied who had actually given me business or touched my life in some significant way over the last ten years. I can't tell you, in words, how shocked I was to learn that there were only 87! Eighty-seven out of 5,365! How could I have missed that? My strategy was to run all over the country giving out little pieces of Bob to thousands of people, and the return, in actual business, was nil. Don't get me wrong. I enjoy meeting people, but I should have been spending more time investing in the 87 who were actually impacting my life in significant ways.

When I discovered the "100/40 Strategy," everything changed. Now, I focus a larger portion of my time interacting with the people on my "100 List," and the rest takes care of itself.

The celebrated *New York Times* best-selling book *The Tipping Point*, by Malcolm Gladwell, outlines a principle called the "Law of the Few," which says there are certain types of people who are unusually helpful at spreading ideas. He calls them "connectors, mavens, and salespeople." Connectors have lots of acquaintances. Mavens are experts on products or technology and continually share their ideas with others. Salespeople are magnetic individuals who are principally successful at persuasion. What's amazing when you reconnect with your *"Who"* is that you find most of us already have these "connectors, mavens, and salespeople" in our "100 List." They're ready to assist us on our journey in life, yet many continually fail to recognize them.

Even Jesus walked side by side every day with his small group of 12 friends and today everyone knows his name. It's more than two thousand years later and he's still doing deals! Out of the 12 there were 3 close and 1 best friend. Do you know your special 12, 3, and 1? Are you actively engaged in investing in them? Or have you been doing what I used to do? Spreading yourself too thin, thinking more is better? Listen to me. Picture me standing up on my chair waving my arms and

USE YOUR *"WHO"* TO MARKET YOU

Those are my principles, and if you don't like them . . . well, I have others.

—GROUCHO MARX

There are unchanging principles that govern the natural world. These principles are so reliable they've become laws. The law of gravity ensures that what goes up must come down. The law of aerodynamics governs every plane that flies. The law of inertia keeps moving things moving and still things still. There are also unchanging principles at work in the world of relationships. Like the laws of nature, these relationship principles have proven to be so reliable that they, too, could qualify as laws. Take, for example, the law of comedy. You know that one, right? This law guarantees that every time Jerry Seinfeld or Chris Rock stands and speaks in front of an audience, people are going to laugh. It's a law. Don't fight it.

When it comes to connecting with your dreams and goals, the golden rule is *"Who"* always comes before *"What."* Both are essential, but the choice of where to start is of paramount importance. Starting with *"Who"* rather than *"What"* will send you in the right direction and, more importantly, will keep you focused on what's truly essential.

In my first sales job, with the Carnation Company, my company car was a beat-up old Rambler that looked like a refugee from a figure-8 race. It had lots of dents, faded paint, no wheel covers; it was a perfect Blues Brothers car. I sold a wide assortment of canned products to the food service side of schools, hospitals, and restaurants. Each day, I had to cook up some product and put it in a thermos for my buyers to sample.

Mrs. Perkins, who could've played the part of Aunt Bea of *Mayberry,* was the buyer at a school district in Lubbock, Texas. I arrived at 6:15 a.m. carrying a large product bag, fully looking the part of the dorky salesman. I was twenty-two years old and so intensely focused on selling what I had in my bag that it never dawned on me that Mrs. Perkins might not actually enjoy chili for breakfast with her morning coffee. When she saw me begin to unscrew the lid, the kind Mrs. Perkins said, "Son, please don't open that thermos. It's six-fifteen in the morning!" As I fumbled around in my bag to find a promo shot of the product, she began to ask me about my family. I found myself feeling very much at ease in her presence. For the next forty-five minutes Mrs. Perkins talked about her family, especially her grandchildren. I was getting a lesson in patience when it came to sales. She was so nice to me that day that I began to look forward to our next visit, hoping, of course, that somewhere along the line she'd buy some of my product. I closed my bag preparing to leave, and, after a few more cordial remarks, I thanked her for taking the time to meet with me. As I headed toward the door I heard her say, "Bob, aren't you forgetting something?" I turned around looking for whatever I had left behind. She said, "I'll take one hundred cases of chili." Overwhelmed, I ran over and hugged her! It was my first sale, and I learned a lesson that has stayed with me my whole life. It wasn't my pitch, my product, or even my company that landed my first big sale. It was my willingness to listen.

I thought I was being smart by following the "letter of the law" outlined in the company sales manual. But obviously, it wasn't very smart at all to believe someone would actually want to eat chili out of a thermos at 6:15 a.m. Mrs. Perkins taught me a valuable lesson about the Power of *"WHO!"* Time has taught me, she was a lot smarter than my sales manager.

It's all about relationships

Almost everyone likes to start with anything but *"Who"* because they're more comfortable with the technical than the relational. They'd rather work on their résumés or read books on interviewing techniques than develop their own *"Who,"* those special relationships with the people who care about them the most. So, they take personality and aptitude tests, conduct extensive research in their desired field, attend seminars and lectures, and expend a lot of mental energy thinking these will lead them to discover their destiny or next assignment in life. Occasionally, they come up with a general idea about an industry they like or type of job they believe they would enjoy. Then they make lists of companies that operate in their field of interest and blast off résumés and letters to "Dear Sir," "To Whom It May Concern," or "Dear Recruiter/ Staffing Manager." After all that work they fire off e-mail blasts to just any *"Who."* Does that work? This is so important I'm standing back up on my chair with my arms spread out saying, "Big Mistake!"

They might as well buy a lottery ticket. E-mail résumés sent in a nonrelational way are called *junk mail*. It's spam and you just got deleted. Why? Who has time to read it? Nobody! They didn't even take the time to come up with an actual person's name. Even if they did, it's not much better than grabbing a name randomly out of a company directory or phone book. Big Mistake!

Ask yourself, should you spend all your precious time studying, researching, and meditating on the *"What"* without having a plan for the *"Who"*?

We all need bridges

The *"What"* in life will take you only so far. Sooner or later you'll come to a chasm you can't cross without someone's help. That's the *"Who"* I'm talking about. People are "bridges" you must cross to get where you want to go. You can stay on the other side if you choose, but you need to understand that your *"What"* will never come into play until your *"Who"* brings you across.

Elvis Presley, with all his raw talent, would never have become the "King of Rock 'n' Roll" without his manager, Tom Parker, acting as his bridge to the world of show business. Billy Graham would never have become the world's greatest evangelist without William Randolph Hearst acting as his bridge to the American public by promoting Reverend Graham in his newspapers. Tiger Woods became the preeminent, dominating force in golf because his father was the bridge who acted as his lifelong coach and mentor. In the same way, you will need people to be your "bridge." The old saying "No man is an island" is true. There is no such thing as a "self-made" person.

Step one: marketing you

If you're going to succeed, you will need to have a basic grasp of how marketing works. Corporations look at marketing as building a bridge between what their company is going to sell and who their potential customers are. Before they introduce their products to the public, they'll do the necessary research and planning on how to successfully market those products.

They'll consider packaging, pricing, messaging, advertising, distribution, sales, and customer service. Everything will be designed to meet the requirements and desires of the customer. The smart people know that the best products aren't sold; they are bought.

You're a product—a brand that needs to be marketed correctly. The old way of "networking" is like a broken-down bridge you can't get across. It may get you a job, but it won't get you your Dream Job. If you're just looking for a job, you should probably be reading another book. Many people think that an awesome cover letter and substantive experience listed in your résumé will get an immediate callback. Wrong! People who send unsolicited résumés usually get the same result—zero. Why? Because the hiring executive (or dream facilitator) glanced at your cover letter only for about one second to see if it was personally addressed to them. Next, they checked to see if a friend referred you. If they don't see a familiar name, you get tossed or filed. The reason is simple—they don't know you!

Senior executives are cynical of résumés. They all look alike, and many have been written by the same marketing and outplacement firms. Most executives believe résumés are embellished (imagine that), and since people would never tell anything bad about themselves, the value of résumés is discounted. If they don't know you, know a friend who knows you, or if you're not the well-known expert in their field, don't be surprised when they pass you over. Going after your Dream Job requires a different strategy than just looking for a job. It's as different as bass fishing is to deep-sea fishing. Landing the "big one" begins by having one of your "100 List" friends "tee you up." That means they're willing to give you a stellar referral to one of their *"Who"* friends. Because of your friend, you get access to a specific executive in a specific company who has the power to open just the right door to your Dream Job.

Universities hire my firm to confidentially bring them the top basketball and football coaches to interview. Finding the head basketball coach for a major NCAA Division 1A school is typical of the kind of work we do. In the past these institutions didn't hire executive recruiters. But now with all the paparazzi, sports talk shows, and newspaper writers trying to scoop each other with news of the candidates, it's very important to universities to keep the interview process off the radar. My job in executive search is to go behind the scenes and find out if a particular coach would be interested. If the coach says yes, I then review their contract information and buyouts, make sure the university can attract them, handle references and education verification, and most of all, interview the candidate with an eye toward determining if there's a good cultural fit with the institution.

STEP TWO: INTERVIEWING STRATEGY

When it comes to the interview stage, each of my candidates enters totally confident that he/she is the best for the job, and, of course, that's the right attitude. However, I see these same highly talented and competent individuals shoot themselves in the foot by making one or more of the following *four* "deadly mistakes." Each one kills any chance of landing the Dream Job because they all take the focus off the *"Who"* and emphasize the *"What."*

1. *Too Much Information*

Some coaches believe the deciding factor in an interview is what's known as the "Book." The "Book" is the volumes of information, materials, and experience they can present with regard to their career. These candidates place all their emphasis on creating an in-depth document that outlines their professional philosophy, recruiting style, wins and losses, staff, practice routine, offense, defense, community relations, graduation rates, etc. They leave no stone unturned when it comes to their all important *"What."* They leave this Godzilla-size book for the committee members. It has twenty-three tabs on everything you can imagine! Is anybody on the committee actually going to read the "Book"? Of course not! No one has the time. Six tabs are enough. The materials you present should be organized simply and concisely, tailored toward meeting the committee's needs. People who make the mistake of giving "too much information" need to realize they got the interview in the first place because someone liked them and was already convinced about their qualifications. At this stage, the interview is really about meeting you and getting to know you on a personal level.

> **{!}** People hire people, not résumés.

The committee members want to see and be convinced that you possess the kind of passion and leadership qualities needed to succeed in this important role. News flash! The best-qualified candidates on paper don't always win. Employers look for personal qualities that transcend technical expertise. They're more impressed with you when you can tell your story in a relaxed, confident, and visionary style. Displaying a good sense of humor also helps.

When an interviewer asks a question, give a succinct answer. If you hold the conversation for too long—you lose. Don't overcommunicate with "too much information."

2. *The Mortar Attack*

The next common error a candidate makes is to believe that bombarding people with endorsements will get them their Dream Job. They'll have a bunch of acquaintances make a lot of phone calls on their behalf to the person doing the hiring. I call this launching a "mortar attack" on the client. Big Mistake! It's like shooting a mosquito with a shotgun. It's overkill. The client isn't stupid and soon realizes that most of the people calling actually have no real experience with the candidate. Soon they become annoyed with all the interruptions of the "mortar attack," because it begins to feel like what it is—manipulation.

One of the biggest names in college basketball coaching called me on behalf of a candidate. The only problem was that the big-time coach mispronounced the guy's name that he supposedly knew so well. Ouch! I wasn't impressed. As a matter of fact, it had the opposite effect. Pick your references carefully. Having people who barely know you make calls on your behalf is risky. It's a potential minefield simply because you don't know how the people you're using as references are being perceived on the other end. So, tread lightly and choose wisely. If you happen to know the hiring person's best friend or boss/mentor—now that's gold! Doing the research to find out if you know any friends or associates of the hiring executive is time well spent.

There's another unseen danger with references. Having worked with thousands of candidates during the last twenty-nine years, I can confidently predict that if you give me six or seven references, one of them will trash you. It really hurts to know that the person who trashed you is a name you gave as a reference. That one bad reference could cost you your Dream Job. Make sure that all the names you provide as personal references come only from your *"Who"* friends.

3. *Emphasizing* "What" *Not* "Who"

The third major mistake candidates make is believing that the interview is all about them and their *"What."* They lead with their résumé, their qualifications, and their record of achievements. In doing so, they miss the opportunity to vitally connect with the people in the organization conducting the interview. The secret key when it comes to Dream Jobs is to remember it's all about *"Who"!* Do your research. Find out who will be in the room doing the interview. Knowing something about them personally and then strategically mentioning it during the interview is always impressive. Having knowledge of their accomplishments or what they wrote about in previous articles or said in interviews shows you've done your homework and that you care.

An interview can come down to "one thing." It could be that conversation you brought up about a common friend, the interviewer's hobby or family, or some piece you turned up in your research that makes a connection between you and the hiring executive. It's obvious you have to have the qualifications, but after that—it's all about *"Who"!*

■ The "I Like You" Factor

It's amazing to me that some people don't know when they've already won. They'll keep talking about their *"What"* even after the interviewer is ready to hand them the contract. Know when to keep quiet, know when to back off and let the other people in the room work for you. It's what I call the "I like you" factor. Simply put, this principle states that when a person likes you, they'll want to help you succeed. Behind the scenes, they will tell others they like you. I see it all the time. If the client likes you in the interview, they'll be less concerned about your weaknesses and let you off the hook by not asking tough follow-up questions. But if they don't know you or are neutral on the "I like you" factor, they'll question you in more detail and might become skeptical of your potential success and fit. People like doing business with people they like! The "I like you" factor is all about *"Who"!* Don't misunderstand; I'm in no way diminishing hard work, great skills, or impressive accomplishments. What I'm saying is that when all the elements of *"What"* are basically equal between candidates (as they often are), *"Who"* becomes the critical factor. No matter how qualified you might be, remember, no one wants to hire or promote someone they suspect might be a relational pain in the neck.

The "I like you" factor enters into the equation because of your *"Who."* The more people like you, the better chance you have at landing your dream. People will open doors for you simply because they prefer you. They'll hire you because they believe others will like you as well. So smile.

Smile a Little Smile for Me

The choice to smile is really a breakthrough technique, because it automatically distinguishes you from most everybody else. I can tell you firsthand that many people lose job opportunities simply because they didn't bring a smile to the interview. Clients have often told me afterward they had an "uneasy feeling" about the candidate because the person looked unhappy or too serious. The candidate missed a golden opportunity simply by not smiling (being too uptight).

Just smiling can actually change the atmosphere of an entire room. When you bring to the table a positive attitude accompanied by a smile, you take on a personal glow that causes good things to happen:

- Everything looks brighter.

- Your presentation looks more impressive.

- You look better in what you're wearing.

- Your interaction is enhanced.

- You signal to everyone that you're confident even in the midst of difficult circumstances.

A genuine smile from a pleasant heart causes those around you to feel at ease. When people feel welcomed and valued by you, they relax and begin to give you the treasure of their trust. So, smile! Trust me; I do this for a living.

4. *Wanting It Too Badly*

We have all been there at one time or another, whether it's wanting to make the team, get that part in the play, having a romantic relationship, or landing the Dream Job. If you show you want something too much, your odds of getting it go down significantly. Dogs, dates, and prospective bosses all can sense this overanxious desire. If you want something or someone too much, you can end up sabotaging yourself. It could be the nervous look, the bouncing leg, or the overly aggressive approach. Regardless of what gives you away, it becomes obvious to everyone around you that you're too emotionally invested. Wanting something too much changes your natural personality and ends up making you look *weak*.

One of my candidates for a CEO role did a great job in the interview. He was well prepared, touched on all the right things, and was perceived by the client as a very strong and viable choice for the role. After the interview I told him to relax. My client told me he had performed superbly. However, the process was going to take a little longer than normal, since the board of directors planned to meet with several other candidates before making a final decision. I told him to be patient and hang in there. But . . . he wanted it too much. He called me over and over to ask how he did in the interview and to find out if I had any more feedback from the client. Not satisfied with my assurances, he decided to bypass me and started calling the client directly. Not once, but over and over! Big Mistake! It was confusing and a huge turn-off to everyone involved. All of a sudden he was out when he would have been in! His was the classic case of "shooting yourself in the foot." He got caught up in *"What"* and forgot about *"Who."*

HERE ARE A FEW BONUS TIPS TO TAKE INTO YOUR DREAM JOB INTERVIEW

▪ You must come prepared. Author and renowned motivational speaker Jeffrey Gitomer nails it when he says, *"Prepare to win, or lose to someone who is!"*

▪ Having great references, endorsements, and testimonials are your most powerful allies. When someone else says you're great, you are! So choose your references carefully and you won't have to toot your own horn.

▪ The interview is usually won or lost in the first five minutes. Here is a great secret: every person carries their own, unique personal environment that is invisibly transmitted to everyone in the room. So, when you walk in, bring your very best, positively charged attitude. Be careful here. If you're faking it, people will intuitively sense you're not for real. Don't sit down until you're invited. Instead, move steadily forward around the room to each person, shaking hands as you go and totally focusing on each individual you meet. Don't let your eyes wander from the person you're addressing. Remember, you're seeking to "connect." But don't force it. When it comes time for you to address the people in the room, be prepared to make a winning opening statement. Use word pictures so others can see your vision. If you don't have a vision and aren't prepared to present it with clarity and passion, then you shouldn't be in the room to begin with.

▪ There are four things a potential employer or prospective client thinks about when they first meet you. These are questions that go through their mind: (1) Do I know you? (2) Do I like you? (3) Do you understand my needs? and (4) Are you the best for me and my particular situation? Interestingly, all four questions involve the *"Who"* factor. Consequently, a strategy of finding one person from your *"Who"* World who is friends with the decision maker and would give you a positive reference before your meeting is time well spent.

▪ Ninety-four percent of the time, a candidate wins the interview over others of equal or sometimes even better talent simply because the interviewer (committee) liked you. But if you're trying too hard, you might make the mistake of interrupting someone who is already speaking. During an interview, smiles and laughter help create a friendly, nonthreatening environment and send the signal that you're relaxed and welcoming rather than guarded and argumentative.

▪ Focus on that "one thing!" Each job has at least one key technical requirement for success. Know what that is before you get there.

▪ Tell stories (but keep them short). Most of the time people enjoy hearing about accomplishments wrapped in personal stories. Great storytelling leaves people with a better understanding of the message being portrayed. Stories are comforting in an interview setting. However, it takes wisdom to know when to speak and when not to speak. Long-winded answers usually have a negative effect. Brevity is always the best policy.

▪ Be authentic. Anything less—you lose.

THE FINAL DIFFERENCE

When there are two great candidates for a Dream Job, it's not always talent that makes the difference. It's vitally important you understand this. Yes, qualifications count. Yes, the facts might favor you. But what you need to know is life isn't always fair, and important decisions at this level are rarely, if ever, made with a scorecard mentality.

So, what makes the final difference? It comes down to personal character qualities that transcend all the technical:

- Confidence carried lightly

- Leadership that engenders trust

- Passion that's contagious

- Humor without derision

- Integrity without guile

- Character that commits

- Loyalty that holds on

- Desire that dreams

- Interest that increases knowledge

Bringing your positive, energized environment with you to an interview will make you shine.

MIRRORING, MENTORS, AND A "PERSONAL BOARD OF DIRECTORS"

No matter how good you are, you're going to lose one-third of your games. No matter how bad you are, you're going to win one-third of your games. It's the other third that makes the difference.

—TOMMY LASORDA

Mirroring success

If you grew up without a guiding force/mentor, don't be too concerned. It's not a dream killer. There are plenty of people who had to overcome tremendous deficits and move past seemingly insurmountable obstacles to achieve greatness.

Ray Charles started out in life way behind the power curve. He was born in the Deep South in 1930. He was black, blind, and an orphan. He was definitely not voted "most likely to succeed" in his high school annual or offered a scholarship to Harvard. But he had an extraordinary musical gift and was determined to succeed. His idol was Nat King Cole. Ray began to model himself after the great singer-musician while at the same time developing his own unique style that eventually catapulted him into incredible success that brought him fame and fortune. Ray Charles became an internationally recognized musical icon. But early on he allowed himself to mirror someone else's success, and it served him well.

Mirroring is a very effective tool for aspiring dream seekers. It's basically imitating, copying, or mimicking someone who is already wildly successful at the same thing you aspire to.

You've actually been mirroring since you were a kid. You watched and copied your mom and dad, your big sister, brother, coach, teacher—how they walked, talked, acted, and played, as well as what they valued. As you grew older, your attention was drawn toward others you admired: actors, athletes, musicians, artists, entrepreneurs, etc. Here is one of life's most powerful principles:

> {!} We move in the direction of our focus.

For example, if you dream of becoming a TV anchor, you will find yourself in front of a mirror copying the style of your favorite anchors and pretending you're them. If you want to play guitar like Stevie Ray Vaughn or Eric Clapton, you'll spend a lot of time learning chords and "licks." You won't mind practicing so you can learn how to play like them. A friend of mine, Craig James, former Super Bowl, all-pro halfback, told me that upon retirement he practiced hour after hour in front of his mirror believing he was on ESPN. He wanted the role so badly he could *see* it! He would tape his intros, and time them, and do it all over again until he mastered it. When asked later what it was like when he auditioned and won the ESPN desk role with Lee Corso and Chris Fowler, he said, "Well, it was just like I saw it in the mirror!"

Mirroring starts by hearing about or seeing someone who

is already doing what you want to do. When that happens, something inside you goes, "Wow, that's it!" You start thinking to yourself, "I can do that. I'd be good at that. I bet I can do it even better if I practice!" When things like this begin to happen, you need to know you're looking at a road map, a blueprint, a model of what could be.

One of the top success writers in the country is Brian Tracy. He talks about the "Law of Attraction" in his best-selling book *Maximum Achievement*. Brian says, *"You are a living magnet. You invariably attract into your life people and situations in harmony with your dominant thoughts."*

Mirroring works in much the same way. But it isn't as easy as it may sound. Craig James will tell you that it takes "want to" coupled with action. In other words, desire that leads to doing. That's why it's so important to love your job. Otherwise, you won't put in the work it takes to become great at it! The proof is in your pursuit. It's called passion. The intensity and dedication of your pursuit are the level of your passion. It takes study and practice to become skilled in the dream you're pursuing. When you find that job you love and are willing to pay the price to become the absolute best at it, then your own unique style and genius will begin to take over and create a new story line that's even better than the one you mirrored. So, be clear about what you want, and mirror the best!

CHOOSE MENTORS

Some people give themselves way too much credit when they win and way too much condemnation when they lose. In reality it all comes down to that "other third" in life. These are those special moments and choices that make all the difference in life. That's where mentors come in. Dictionary.com describes a mentor as *"a wise and trusted counselor or teacher."*

These are people who've been there before and have

already achieved the results we desire. Many years ago Bruce Springsteen was just another unknown musician. But he received some mentoring from a few musician friends who were already successful and willing to share their knowledge and experience with him. As a result he made some important decisions about his associations, and that changed everything. The people he surrounded himself with became known as the E Street Band, and the rest is music history.

Mentors make a difference. The people with whom you associate will, in large measure, determine the level of your success or failure in life. Remember, everyone is an influencer.

So, whom should I pick as a mentor? Well, look around you. Who would you say that you admire and respect? Who has always impressed you with their creativity and insightfulness? Is it your manager, or your boss's boss? Is it a successful neighbor, member of your country club, charity, or even an old member of your fraternity/sorority? Maybe it's a top executive in a different part of the company, or a banker, professor, consultant, or legal adviser? What about a recently retired CEO who has lots of experience to pass on? Are they willing to offer some guidance and assistance? Why not ask them? Don't be shy. Even if they say no, and they probably won't—I promise they will still be very flattered. So go deep into your "100 List" for your mentors. If one of the names you desire isn't a *"Who"* today, who says they won't be tomorrow?

CREATE A "PERSONAL BOARD OF DIRECTORS"

There is a well-known proverb that says:

> **{!}** Plans fail for lack of counsel, but with many advisers they succeed.

There are many more paths that lead to failure than there are that lead to success. The main reason so many people continue to take the paths that lead to failure is because those paths are well worn. They're wider and easier. The paths to failure offer less resistance. None of us can see every possibility coming our way, so we need a self-protective strategy in place, like a firewall that protects computers from destructive viruses that try to sneak in undetected and wreak havoc. We've all seen the mistakes of many high-profile people that result in embarrassment and public humiliation. I've come to believe one of the very best strategies you can implement to achieve maximum protection is to create your own "personal board of directors."

This strategy ties in directly with your "100 List," where your top advisers reside. These are your inner circle of trusted friends. So, who makes this list, and how many members do I pick to be on my board? There are *seven* categories that make up your "personal board of directors."

1. *Mom/Dad.* There is a blessing promised in the Bible to those who honor their mothers and fathers. It says that if you do, "It will go well with you, and your days will be long on the earth." This amazing yet simple promise is often overlooked. But it's wise to have one of your board members be your mom or dad. Pick one. If, however, you're one of the many people without a healthy Mom/Dad relationship, look around for a person willing and able to fill that role. It could be a grandparent, uncle, aunt, or even an older friend with whom you relate as a parent figure.

2. *Mate.* This could mean different people at different times in your life. In college, your mate could be a close friend or that "special someone." At some point, your mate could mean your spouse. If so, it's beneficial to

understand that the goal of marriage is oneness. "The two shall become one flesh." With about half of the country getting divorced, oneness is obviously not being achieved by many couples. In a marriage of oneness, your spouse is your most powerful ally.

3. *Best Friend.* Your best friend needs to be someone who is loyal and courageous. A best friend is someone who has a special discernment about you and is available when you need them. Choose the one friend who will tell you what you truly need to hear, the thing that others wouldn't feel comfortable telling you. Best friends cut right to the bone. They nail you because they have an "All Access" pass to the backstage of your life. They are free to speak without overanalyzing because they speak the language of authentic friendship.

4. *Legal Counsel.* You've probably already heard the old cliché many times: "The person who represents himself in legal matters has a fool for a client." There are people who are really good at this stuff. They've studied hard for years, passed the bar and work in the legal profession everyday. Do yourself a favor, when it comes to legal matters rely on knowledgeable experts. If you don't, you run a very high risk of embarrasing yourself and ending up with a bunch of legal knots that could cost a bundle to untangle. The principle is simple: pay a little now and avoid paying a lot later.

5. *Career/Life Coach.* A talented career coach helps you assess the multitude of choices and possibilities available today. This person may assist you in identifying talents/gifts, writing "wow" résumés/cover letters, learning the art of interviewing, as well as giving tips on compensation, contracts, benefits, and branding. A wise and gifted life coach is a tremendous ally who can help keep you grounded emotionally and sometimes spiritually. This person is usually more interested in your character development. A good life coach knows that you may achieve great success and still derail your life because of character flaws that were left unattended. It's wise to have such an individual evaluate your situation on an ongoing basis. Sometimes the career coach and life coach can be the same person. The crucial point is: it's a mistake to think you are smart enough to advise yourself in these important areas. Again, choose wisely. Pick an expert.

6. **Financial Adviser.** Statistics say that 90 percent of the country is not getting financial advice from an expert. I want to give you a **DO** and a **DON'T**.

DO get with someone you trust who you know is competent in this field—someone you can rely on, who has a solid track record of success, whose integrity is impeccable, then take the time needed to get your finances on track.

DON'T try to do this on your own unless you're already very good at it, enjoy it, and intend to diligently spend a lot of time overseeing this strategic area of life. You'll need a strategy for employment income and savings income, and creating passive income.

7. **Spiritual Adviser.** The most common definition of blindness describes a person who cannot see physically. But the word *blind* also means "unwilling or unable to perceive or understand." Each of us is "blind" in some things. We need a wise spiritual adviser to help bring understanding to us in areas of morality and ethics. In tough times it's good to be able to talk and consider the wisdom of our spiritual adviser (pastor, priest, rabbi, or other trusted spiritual counselor).

The point is: identify those individuals on your "100 List" who fit the criteria needed to be on your "personal board of directors." Ask these special individuals if they would be willing to meet with and counsel you a few times a year, as needed, in person or by phone. Always seek the advice of those closest to you—your *"Who"!* These are the people you love and who love you. You trust them because you know they have no selfish agenda. Your happiness and success are important to them.

Note: If you just graduated from college, you may not need your own legal or financial advisers just yet, and if you do, perhaps your parents/key advisers can provide people they trust. However, you *do* need the other board members.

"BOARD MEMBER" REQUIREMENTS

What qualities should you look for in your "personal board of directors"? Start with integrity and authenticity, then move on to unconditional love, loyalty, truthfulness, and, when necessary, even bluntness. If you're about to make a wrong turn in life, these folks will tell you boldly of impending danger. Your "board of directors" should have no agenda, should never play the "yes person" to you, and want nothing in return but your well-being and success. They should be bright, savvy, street smart, and quickly able to assess the pros and cons of a situation and tell you "yea" or "nay" based on facts, not emotions. Choose people with whom you share common core values. Today, more than ever, we need friends who will watch over us and protect us—sometimes from ourselves.

The Bible's book of wisdom speaks about how important it is to have a board like this:

> *"He who walks with wise men will be wise, but the companion of fools shall be destroyed."*
> —PROVERBS 13:20

How important is this concept of having a "personal board of directors"? Let's review a few names that made it into the national press because of their foolish behavior:

Bill Clinton—former president of the United States

Kobe Bryant—NBA superstar

Martha Stewart—TV celebrity/CEO

Michael Vick—NFL quarterback

Britney Spears, Lindsay Lohan, or Paris Hilton—celebrity

Do you think these individuals would have benefited by having a "personal board"? I didn't even mention the host of other actors and actresses involved with drugs, DUI charges, shoplifting, fights, and even divorces after one night. You and I both know this is a long list! These are smart and talented people—what were they thinking? Obviously, they weren't thinking or they wouldn't have made such poor decisions. Where were their *"Who"?*

It's just a little alarming to know you and I are just as vulnerable without our "personal board of directors." It has been very revealing to me over my years as an executive recruiter, in interview after interview, to realize that a significant and differentiating factor of one candidate over the other was the quality of their "personal board" (or lack of them). These important advisers are the ones who helped design, guide, and encourage the successful candidates to believe in themselves, press the outer limits, shoot for the stars, and discover their dreams. It could have been a mom, dad, coach, teacher, or best friend. I consider having a "personal board of directors" to be an absolutely vital strategy for your success in life.

DETOURS VS. "DREAM KILLERS"

Every problem is an opportunity in disguise.

—*OCEAN'S ELEVEN*

It's almost a proverb. Someone gets pumped up about their dreams and goals and begins moving in that direction but encounters a few bumps along the way and gives up, often just before something great was about to happen. Even though they desperately want to succeed, deep in their heart they never really expected them to come true. Discouraged by their apparent failure, they make the one fatal mistake that totally kills the momentum—they quit. It very rarely occurs to the dreamer that what appears to be a dead end might be only a "detour."

Detours take you off the main road into unfamiliar territory. Unexpected turns can disorient you unless you have the rare ability to stay alert and immediately acclimate to your new circumstances. When you hit a detour (and "hit" is the proper expression because that's what it feels like), the first thing you need to realize is that your windshield is a whole lot bigger than your rearview mirror. You can't get back on the old road. That road has run out. It will do you absolutely no good to dwell on the past. Order yourself, "Eyes forward!"

There is a rock-solid rule regarding detours that will help you tremendously while you traverse the bumpy roads of life. I want you to write it down and keep it where you'll see it every day until it becomes a part of you, for it will be a very powerful ally. It's that important. It will give you the power to maintain your equilibrium as you encounter the detours:

> {!} Regard the unknown as friendly and ultimately beneficial.

Remember, a detour is not permanent. It's not the road to your destiny. It's a necessary but temporary side route. Perhaps there are some things you need to acquire or learn. Maybe there's someone you need to meet who holds the key to your destiny and who will help you succeed. A detour could mean you help someone else achieve their goals, and in the process discover some key elements you'll need to accomplish on your own. Learn to view every problem you encounter as "an opportunity in disguise." Don't get angry and don't get discouraged. Remember, the road to success is always under construction.

When you ask most people to name some of the hindrances that keep them from crossing the finish line, the list would very likely include at least a few of these age-old excuses:

1. "I'm just too busy and overcommitted."

2. "I'm fearful someone might find out I'm looking and get me fired."

3. "I haven't written a résumé in years."

4. "I don't have the right kind of people in my network."

5. "I don't have a network."

6. "I don't have the right education."

There are lots of garages where you can park your dreams. But it's dark in there, you can't see, and over time your dreams gather dust. So resolve now never to use excuses.

"DREAM KILLERS"

Some "dream killers" are more insidious than others because they can fly under your radar and attack you while you're still getting dressed for battle. The good news is you can have control over these hindrances, but you have to first recognize where they're coming from when they attack.

So, let's expose the four major "dream killers" and deal with each one.

They are:

■ Self-talk

■ "Double-Mindedness"

■ Lack of Competency (not paying the price)

■ Lack of Authenticity (not letting the real "you" shine)

1. Self-talk

I've been hearing voices telling me . . .
        "I can't."
        "I'm probably not good enough."

"I'll never find the money to start that."

"I'm too late."

"I'm too old."

"I'm too young."

"It's too risky."

Have you ever heard any of these voices? Where do they come from? Are you going to continue to allow them to influence you? I hope your answer is an emphatic no! Every time one of these little "gremlins" makes its way into your head, ask yourself: "Who told you that?"

One day I was chatting with my dad in his office. Actually, I wasn't chatting; I was complaining that my business was off and things in general seemed a bit bleak. Now my dad was one of the wisest men I've ever known. He allowed me to complain till all that junk was out in the open. Most of my complaints were little worries that *could* come true but, in reality, never happened. After listening patiently, he lowered his head, looked over his glasses, and asked, "Are you done? Is that everything that's bugging you? Hmm . . . now those are some *big* problems."

I could tell he was giving me a hard time. But then he surprised me. He told me he had the answer to my problems on a three-by-five card in the right-hand corner of his desk drawer.

"Huh?"

He seemed serious, though. He beckoned me with his finger to come around to his side of the desk and take a look. With eyebrows slightly raised and my eyes never losing contact with Dad, I slowly walked around to the drawer and pulled it open. There, lying on the bottom of the drawer was the three-by-five card. I reached in, pulled it out, and turned it over. The card simply read *"IT'S NOT TRUE!"* Initially, I didn't get it. "What's not true?" I asked.

"You know, Bob," he began. "When I fight thoughts that gnaw at me about various situations and circumstances, I pull out that little three-by-five card and just think about its simple, yet profound message. Just three short words.

"Most of the time," he explained, "the clamor that goes on in our minds—those silly, pestering, negative thoughts—just don't pan out. In other words, 'IT'S NOT TRUE.' I guess some of them could become true at some point in the future but right now they're just annoying little thoughts. If you let those thoughts continue to torment you, then it's possible they could take root and grow up to be big thoughts, and that would be disastrous for you. But, why would you do that? Why would you want to continue to listen to that kind of negative self-talk?"

I had developed a bad habit of living either in the future, worrying about circumstances looming ahead, or living in the past, tormenting myself over things I saw in the rearview mirror of my life. Even now, I can clearly hear him saying, "It's not true." But then Dad asked me an even tougher question. "Bob, do you know what is true?"

I couldn't help but smile as he spoke.

"You're a treasure chest filled with amazing talents, gifts, capabilities, dreams, aspirations, originality, passion, power, encouragement, and joy. You have been designed for maximum performance. You can choose to turn off that negative self-talk and choose, instead, to think positive, creative, life-giving thoughts. Or, you can let the tormenting self-talk have its way with you. It's up to you. You get to choose."

I felt manipulated after I began to think about those three simple words written on a plain three-by-five card. I had been anxious, worried, and bothered. As a matter of fact, I had allowed this to happen quite often with regard to my dreams and goals about the future.

I took a walk to reflect on that conversation. My blood was pumping, and my pace was brisk. But after a few minutes out in the fresh air, I slowed down and quieted my mind. I came to the only reasonable conclusion I could. Dad was right. "It's not true!"

Have you ever found yourself in a negative conversation

with yourself! This self-talk needs to be filtered like spam. Very often it's just a lot of intrusions attempting to distract you and clog up your thinking. Delete it! Stay focused on the target. Keep set in the direction of your dream. It's probably a good idea to be a little tough on yourself when it comes to putting a stop to the negative, inner babble that says, "You're not good enough," "You're inferior," or "You don't have what it takes."

Negative "self-talk" is an assault on your dreams. Don't put up with it! Most people are so accustomed to it they don't even notice its intrusion. They let it sneak in and ruin their potential for success by causing them to quit too soon. Self-discipline and self-control begin with controlling your own negative self-talk. So, take this bull by the horns and bring it down. Because if you don't, it will defeat you and leave you paralyzed from the neck up. Next time you start believing the lies, just stop and hear me asking, "Who told you that?" And then tell yourself, "IT'S NOT TRUE."

2. *"Double-Mindedness"*

> *In every old person is a young person wondering—what happened?*
> —TERRY PRATCHETT (BEST-SELLING AUTHOR)

"What happened?" I hear this too often in executive search. A candidate who thought the job already was won is caught totally off guard when it goes to someone else. "What happened?" is also something you hear a lot from people in their latter years when they talk about that dream that somehow slipped away. Both types started off well, but life throws them for a loss when they encounter the second of my four major "dream killers"—"double-mindedness."

dou·ble-mind·ed—adjective
wavering or undecided in mind.
—DICTIONARY.COM

In other words, it's an unstable state of mind that sends self-defeating signals to others around you, like (beep-beep):

■ "Don't pick me, I'm confused."

■ "Can't you see I'm not ready to make a decision?"

■ "I'd like this opportunity but—I dunno. Should I? Can I?"

■ "Look at me—I'm a deer caught in your headlights!"

Every day people bring this second hindrance with them to work, to meetings, to personal relationships, and, yes, to auditions and interviews. Of course, companies, committees, agents, human resource executives, dates, etc. react to that quizzical look and that negative vibe in much the same way. They back away.

■ The Man with Two Heads

I recently conducted an athletic director search in which a candidate had two excellent job opportunities from which to choose. One was a role he clearly wanted: AD at a midmajor university near his wife's aging parents. It was a perfect fit for him personally as well as professionally. But just when he was about to focus on that Dream Job, a much larger institution came calling and diverted his attention. He knew he was a long shot for the more prestigious job, but even being considered for such a position had him drooling and his ego inflating. He decided to go for both! This candidate allowed himself to be lured into the trap of "double-mindedness." His thinking became clouded. His schedule was already insanely hectic. It would be like a basketball player in an important game trying to dribble two balls at the same time while running at full speed down the court. Both balls get stolen by the opposing team. This man's loyalties got split trying to win both AD roles and his "double-mindedness" ended up costing him both jobs.

Too many job seekers fall prey to this hindrance of "double-mindedness." I later had the opportunity to talk informally with individuals on both university committees that interviewed the candidate.

The larger school, the one with the bigger, more prestigious job, commented that he looked disconnected in the interview, wasn't specific on goals, strategies and vision, and seemed surprisingly nervous and stiff. In fact, several committee members stated that "even though on paper he looked to be a great fit, in person he just never connected with us."

Just a week earlier, the candidate had felt very confident. But when I spoke with him after the interview to get his view of how it went, he told me he should have prepared better. But he was just too busy doing his job and, of course, also preparing for the interview with the other school. He told me when he first went in for the interview, he felt overwhelmed by the size of the committee. There were no familiar, smiling faces. The group looked less inviting and more serious than he had anticipated. All of a sudden, he said, it felt like a CNN investigative interview. A wave of fear came over him, and his negative self-talk kicked in with questions like "What am I doing here?" "Am I really ready for a job this size?" "Can I do the things necessary to help this school at this time?"

Wham! He became very nervous and began to lose confidence. His body language went rigid. He was thinking so many different and conflicting thoughts during the interview that he just began to mentally shut down. He couldn't hear the "heart" of the questions being posed to him.

Since he was straddling the fence between two jobs, he was never able to focus on just the one. Instead of walking in prepared and confident with a clear plan, he came "double-minded." Guess what? Ding! He was out!

His next job interview didn't go well, either. This was the one he was meant for, the one that both he and his wife really wanted. His approach was just the opposite from his first interview. He was overconfident, thinking he could waltz in, wing it, and get the job. He already knew most of the committee by name. But what he didn't know was that, instead of walking into a room full of supportive friends, he was now entering a room full of people who had cooled toward him. Two important components had come into play that weren't part of the equation at the beginning of the search.

First, members of the search committee found out he had interviewed for another job. That alone let some air out of their sails toward him. Second, they had interviewed four other candidates, and, for the first time, the committee began to entertain the notion there were, indeed, other highly qualified individuals they really liked. His stock was going down rapidly. Unfortunately, he was not able to win them back during the interview. Once again—ding! He was dropped. The committee later commented to me he really didn't seem to want the job. Although he actually did, he had waited too long to make up his mind. As a result, he didn't have the time to develop a strategy that would convince the committee. Also, the four other candidates were clearly qualified for the role and were extremely impressive. They arrived armed with stories, specific examples, and creative ideas about how they could make a difference. They knew going in they were underdogs in this race, so they prepared effectively and had ready answers for the hard questions they knew the savvy committee members would throw at them. When the time came for the final interview, the bar had been raised significantly by the competing candidates. When our "double-minded" man waltzed in unprepared to show the committee a specific plan, a defined vision, and a burning passion for the job, he was DOA. What a hard lesson he learned that day.

When "double-mindedness" takes root, it will stop you

from doing the one thing you know you should do to achieve the victory that is meant for you. A confused person will always appear weaker than the resolute, single-minded individual.

In the words of that great philosopher Yogi Berra:

> **{!}** "If you don't know where you're going, you might end up someplace else."

In other words, if you can't make a clear choice, then someone else will make the choice for you. Don't go into an interview "double-minded"—you'll lose! Confusion causes a "disconnect" to the point where you become unaware of what's really going on around you. My candidate's first comment to me after finding out he didn't win either role was, "What happened?"

3. *Not Paying the Price*

> *My grandfather once told me that there were two kinds of people: those who do the work and those who take the credit. He told me to try to be in the first group; there was much less competition.*
>
> —INDIRA GANDHI

When people start talking about their dreams and passions, they can get stirred up and excited. Sometimes, they may even get ahead of their competency. I love big dreams. They can't be big enough for me. But I would be remiss if I didn't say there is a hindrance here for many people. Everyone can see the end results of someone's success, but few can comprehend the price they paid for the achievement.

A friend of mine is a top executive in the entertainment world. Each year he takes on a new assistant who travels with him all over the globe. This lucky person gets a chance to see what it's like to negotiate big deals, meet famous people, travel in personal jets, stay at great hotels and resorts, and be celebrated everywhere this executive goes. The only problem, he tells me, is that nine out of ten assistants don't "get it," and the result is they don't get hired permanently at the year's end. They become enamored by the glamour and glitz and start believing they deserve the entitlements of "star treatment" without ever having paid the price of admission. Sorry, real life doesn't work that way.

I had the opportunity to hear Baylor University football great Mike Singletary give a motivational talk to the Baylor basketball team as the season was about to begin. Baylor's outstanding basketball coach, Scott Drew, asked Mike, "When you first came to Baylor, you weren't really expected to make the football team. So, when did you decide you wouldn't just make the team, but you'd be a starter? Not just a starter but an all-conference linebacker? Not just all-conference, but someone who achieves all-American status? Not just all-American, but an NFL player? Not just an NFL player, but an all-pro eight times, going to the Pro Bowl ten times? And finally, not only that, but becoming a Hall of Fame linebacker recognized as one of the 'top three' players to ever play the game at your position? When did you decide all that?" Mike responded, "Day one! When I got to campus the first day, I went immediately to the defensive coach and asked him if he would write down exactly what I needed to do to become the best defensive player who ever played at the university. The coach laughed and said, 'That's nice, Mike, but let's not worry about that just now. How about just trying to make the team?' I wouldn't take that for an answer, so I said, 'Coach, please, write down for me exactly what I have to do, and I'll do it!' The coach was stunned, and I'm not sure he knew exactly what to put on paper." After thinking about it for a couple of days, the coach came back with a list. It was broken into three parts:

1. **Robust Physical Goals.** This would mean lots of training time in the weight room. (If completed, it would make Mike the strongest player on the team.)

2. **Nutrition.** Eating the right foods in the proper amounts and not eating certain other foods.

3. **Study.** Extra time spent in order to understand all facets of Baylor's defensive schemes. (This would require Mike to spend hours and hours watching film on the teams he would face, dissecting their offensive strategies.)

Mike then stopped and told Scott's team: "Everybody wants things and has dreams, but that's not enough if you want to be the best. You have to be willing to pay the price, and to pay such a price, you have to see it first and then be accountable to it. This requires vision and a plan with specific goals written out."

Once Mike saw the plan and the specific goals the coach wrote out for him, he knew it would be tough. There just weren't enough hours for all this plus the study and social aspects of college life. Something would have to give, and it couldn't be his studies. The rest is sports history.

All jobs have competency standards that require a fundamental knowledge, ability, or expertise in a specific subject or skill set. Attaining these basic standards of competence requires a price to be paid. It takes study, practice, and a strong work ethic. The hit TV show *American Idol* showcases painful examples of people who totally disregard the concept of competency. As a result, they face the cutting remarks and quizzical looks of the judges, Randy, Paula, and Simon.

I'll never forget a call I got while conducting the search for the commissioner of baseball. A man called and wanted to apply for the role since he read in the newspaper that I was doing the search.

"Great!" I said. "What do you do?"

"I work for Del Taco," he said.

"Interesting, are you the CEO of the company?" I asked.

"Oh no," he replied, "I work here in Dallas."

I was thinking, "Hmm, Del Taco isn't headquartered in Dallas," so I asked, "Are you the regional president? Because as you know this is a pretty big job."

"No, sir," he said. "I'm the food preparation manager in store #184. But please don't let that fool you, because I really love baseball, and I'm sure I can do a better job than the guy who's been doing it!"

I thanked him and told him to go ahead and send me his résumé. But did he really expect to become commissioner of baseball? It isn't enough just being ambitious, opinionated, and having a heartfelt desire to achieve a dream. One doesn't move from being a second lieutenant to a general without mastering the ranks in between. It takes proven competence and experience to be elevated to any high position. The mistake most people make is thinking you elevate yourself. But that's not how it works. You're elevated by others who believe in you. They recognize your gifting, talent, and competency. They also see in you some personal qualities they like and trust you will be successful. Of course, it's usually helpful to already be working in the field where you would like to succeed. There are exceptions to every rule, but your odds of being the exception are astronomical. Resolve today not to let competency be a hindrance. Start working on your gifts and talents now. Enjoy each step in the learning and growing process and be willing to pay the price.

4. *Lack of Authenticity*

> *Be who you is. Don't try to be who you ain't, cause if you try to be who you ain't, you can't be who you is.*
>
> —TOM DOOLEY

Johnny Cash became an American icon simply because he was one of a kind. He remained true to himself, and it made him authentic. Can you imagine having gone to a Johnny Cash concert expecting to hear the songs he made famous, and, instead, he came out onstage and started singing Ray Charles and Frank Sinatra songs? That would have been absurd. But many people try to do the same thing every day. Instead of being themselves, they try to be someone totally different, and the results are usually disastrous or sadly comical, depending on the circumstances. Big Mistake! There is only one you. There may be lots of people who have influenced you even to the point that you've tried to emulate them, but you're totally unique.

Even Johnny Cash had to learn this same lesson. It happened at his first audition in front of Sam Phillips, founder of Sun Records. Even though Johnny had written some of his own songs, he had no confidence in them, so he chose, instead, to "play it safe" and sing a tired old, worn-out gospel tune that had been sung for many years by several other performers. He didn't get very far into the song before Phillips stopped him and asked, "Do you have anything else?" Johnny was taken aback and asked the man if he had something against religion. Phillips replied with frankness, "Mr. Cash, that old type of gospel music doesn't sell, and I only make records that sell." Then he said something that should be drummed into the head of every person looking for their dream. He told Johnny Cash, "I don't believe you!" When Johnny heard this, he was confused. Most people are. So the man said it again. "I don't believe you." What he was saying was "You're not being authentic. You're not being who you really are. You're mimicking others, trying to be somebody else and you're not very good at it."

Phillips then added, "If you were hit by a truck and you were lying in the street dying and you had time to sing one song—one song that would let God know what you felt about your time here on earth, one song that would sum you up, what would it be?" Just then a light went on and a remarkable thing happened. Johnny Cash remembered *his song*. He began to sing a crude version of "Folsom Prison Blues," and the rest is pop music history.

What a question Sam Phillips asked Johnny Cash that day! It's a good question for all of us. What's your dream? Not your dad's, not your mom's, not anybody else's but your own? What's that "one thing" where your unique talent, gifting, and competency are maximized and showcased? Well, let it shine! Bring it to the interview, because you won't succeed if you're not authentic.

But watch out; there's a danger here. In our competitive society, it's possible to be inauthentic and actually beat out the competition for a job you don't really want. Hey, this is not a game show! This is your life! You'd be amazed at how many talented people make this crucial mistake. Don't wear a mask and get yourself into the position of living several years of your life as a counterfeit just because you "aced" the interview and got the gig.

WILL THE REAL YOU PLEASE STAND UP?

Recently there was a search I was handling for a top executive position, and the leading candidate was a shoe in. Just about everyone expected him to win the job easily. But he came into the interview and flat-out flopped. We had talked before the interview and everything was fine. But when he went into the meeting he was nervous, way too serious and so low key that people almost forgot he was in the room. This was baffling because he is actually a dynamic and charismatic person who usually carries any room he enters. But on this particular day, he was more than just off. He lost his authenticity. He forgot who he was.

He acted like such a different person in the interview that afterward I actually came up to him, shook his hand, and re-introduced myself. "Hello, I'm Bob Beaudine. Could you please tell me who that was in there, because it sure wasn't you?"

His head dropped as he said, "I lost it. I don't know what happened, but I froze." He talked a lot about what had gone wrong but couldn't pin it down.

Fortunately, he did do one thing extremely well in the interview. He had a great *"Who"* moment! It came as natural as breathing to him. It not only caused everyone in the room to warm toward him, but they also got to see his authenticity. What was it? Well, when he had first entered the room, he had a "handshake moment" with each person present. He repeated the process as he left. He didn't just shake hands and move down the line as most candidates do. He spent time with each person patiently listening, thanking them and creating a "connection" that each committee member remembered with fondness. This was who he was. This made such a big impression with everybody, that in the end, even with the bad interview, he got the job.

When we suppress our originality, uniqueness, and authenticity, we lose touch with our source of energy and natural creativity. Do yourself an enormous favor. Don't try to be somebody you "ain't." Celebrate your uniqueness. It's what sets you apart and makes you who you really are.

"MOMENT MAKERS"

The only way to have a friend is to be one!

—RALPH WALDO EMERSON

estiny, disguised as spontaneous moments, has a way of disregarding your current personal agenda to make necessary course corrections. These unexpected, serendipitous interruptions are designed to have the delightful effect of redirecting your trajectory. Sometimes these corrections aren't readily apparent.

Nobody knew that the young man with a beard sneaking on to the lot pretending to work there would one day become the most famous movie director in the world. Eventually, Steven Spielberg got the break he needed and forever changed the course of the motion picture industry. Somewhere along the way, he had a strategic moment with somebody who encouraged him and opened a door for him. Most people can recall a special person who took the time to create a "magic moment" that turned their life around for the better. When someone you admire and respect believes in you, it changes everything.

In the same way, there are people who look up to you. You have the power to open the door to someone's dreams and goals just by believing in them and letting them know it! Creating extraordinary moments doesn't cost us a dime, but I promise—it pays huge dividends!

A MOMENT WITH CHARLIE

My dad would often rave about a man he knew who operated a shoe shine stand at the train station in Philadelphia. Charlie was a stately black man revered by many for his words of wisdom and encouragement. So, when it came time for me to make a trip back East, Dad excitedly said, "Bob, make sure you stop and get a shine from Charlie. Trust me on this. It isn't going to be your normal shoe shine." He smiled at me with that familiar twinkle in his eye and assured me it would be worth the effort.

During the flight to Philly, I thought often about the mysterious shoe shine man named Charlie. Dad sure knew how to stir my sense of wonder. After my business in Philly was completed, I caught a taxi and headed to the train station, still intrigued by my impending encounter. I pushed on the revolving door and walked into the enormous main lobby of the busy 30th Street train station. Immediately to my right, I noticed the unimposing shoe shine stand up against the wall. I'm not sure exactly what I expected to see, but there was no "wow" factor. Everything about this stand was ordinary and unassuming. Maybe I thought it would have lights that travel in motion like those big signs in Times Square. You know— something to make it stand out, grab your attention, and pull you in like a tractor beam on *Star Trek*.

But life often disguises the extraordinary in a plain wrapper. Charlie looked to be in his midseventies, average height and weight, silver gray hair, thin on top, and a mustache. That's when I noticed the one thing that did seem out of the ordinary. There was a line of eight or nine people waiting for their turn in Charlie's chair. You might think with that many people wanting to do business that the old guy might hurry things along. But Charlie was in no hurry. He was the calm at the center of the storm. His motions were measured—not because he was old, but because he was graceful. Still, I couldn't help thinking this was going to take too long, and I was young and impatient with a world to conquer. There were just too many people in line. As I turned to leave, Charlie caught my eye. He smiled broadly and nodded slightly as if to say, "Don't leave." But I kept going. Back outside I began looking for a decent restaurant. Halfway down the block, I noticed I was walking very slowly and feeling a slight tug pulling me back. The tractor beam had returned. I could hear my dad, "You mean to tell me you were right there but couldn't wait a few minutes?" Okay, okay. Within a minute I was back in line. The guy in front of me struck up a conversation. He asked me if I was one of Charlie's regulars. "No," I said matter-of-factly, "this is my first time." He told me that senators, mayors, dignitaries, CEOs, and celebrities came from all over to wait in this same line just to spend three minutes in Charlie's chair. I was excited when it was finally my turn.

"Hello, young man, what's your name?" he asked as I settled in. His voice was calm and smooth like a pond with no ripples. "Bob," I replied quietly. "Mine's Charlie. I am so honored you decided to stay, thank you!" I smiled sheepishly like a schoolboy just caught doing something mischievous. "My, you have a nice smile," he said as he began working on my shoes. "Do you have any children?" "Yes," I said proudly, "I have three beautiful girls." "Oh, I knew it," he said, and smiled brightly. "I bet your three girls are very special. Did I tell you, Bob, that children are a gift from God, and how important it is for you to condition them regularly, just like I'm doing to your shoes, by telling them how much you love them?"

A wave of peace and joy rushed in and swept over me. Suddenly I was engulfed in his world, and I was glad to be there.

"You see, Bob," he continued, "your shoes, if you take care of them, will last you a long, long time and will take care of your feet as you go on your journey. Watch how I put some conditioner on them and then shine them with these old hands of mine. When I'm done, they'll shine so bright it'll make you smile every time you look down at them. Your family and friends are a lot like these shoes of yours, Bob. God has given them to you as gifts, and you need to keep them well conditioned. We need to be hands on with love and care so they don't become worn out and begin to feel useless." He paused for a moment as if he were waiting for a thought to complete itself. Then he looked up at me and said with a smile, "I can sense you take care of those around you." Another pause. "But before you leave, my new friend, I have a gift, a blessing that I would like to give to you. I know you'll like it as you go on your way this morning. May I?"

"Of course," I answered quietly.

"All right then, it goes like this":

*Bob, may you have eyes to see the blessings and wonders
     right in front of you.
May you have ears to hear the sounds of love coming from
     your family and friends.
True friends are treasures, Bob.
May you treasure the gifts you've been given.
And may your eyes be opened to the treasures you've been
     missing.
One final thing, Bob, may you polish and condition each of
     your treasures and cause them to shine.*

Charlie's words hung in the air and suspended me in time. I didn't want my three minutes to end. But, after exchanging good-byes, I was suddenly out of the chair and on my way again. I left with the memory of a moment I would never forget. This was an extraordinary man who had friends all over the world who went out of their way when traveling through Philadelphia just to spend a few minutes in Charlie's chair. Now I understood why nobody minded waiting in his line. Before you get your turn in the chair, you get to witness the remarkable transformation in the ones who go before you. It's also very quiet in that line as people lean in wanting to hear what Charlie is saying. Did I tell you that he doesn't charge anything? No mention is ever made about money. There's an old hat lying on the shoe shine stand where patrons put in whatever they want. And it's not uncommon for those who just stop and listen to also make deposits in the crumpled, old hat.

My dad knew that my encounter with the old shoe shine guru would have a lasting effect on me, and he was right. Oh, what a difference one person with the gift of encouragement can make in the lives of those he encounters. For a few, brief moments, I felt like I was in an episode of *The Twilight Zone* as I sat in Charlie's chair. He created a kind of parallel universe, an island in that stream of life that constantly flowed through Thirtieth Street Station. (Rod Serling would have been proud.) All too soon I was thrust back into the real world but with a better perspective on life.

It makes a difference when you show people you care. I know, because it makes a big difference to me when someone cares for me. Dad passed away a number of years ago, and Mom followed six years later. Our homes were only three blocks apart, and we enjoyed a wonderful, loving relationship. My mom would often call just to see how I was doing. I didn't know how much I enjoyed her checking up on me until there were no more calls.

When you make the extra effort to celebrate, encourage, and help others, it establishes stronger bonds of friendship. Each time you do it, it's an investment that is never wasted. There's a law that governs this principle of encouraging and giving. It's called the "law of reciprocity." Simply put, this law states that when you do something good for another person, it actually creates a desire in them to reciprocate. They want to do good back to you. When you do something extra for people, they never seem to forget it and will always try to find a way to balance the equation.

A MOMENT WITH ARNIE

My dad loved to play golf, and his hero was the great Arnold Palmer. When I was about seven years old, Dad began taking me to watch the King of Golf in tournaments all over the country. We would both often comment on what it would be like to play a round with him. It was just a dream. But be careful what you're dreaming, because one day your dreams might be dreaming you.

This incredible dream happened because I was willing to help a friend with his résumé during a critical time in his life. Things had not gone well for a while, and he was feeling vulnerable. He credited the time and encouragement I was able to give him as a key component that opened the door for his later success. He called to thank me and wanted to see what he could do for me. I was happy just seeing him happy. I told him there was no need to reciprocate, but he insisted he wanted to give something back. It just so happened that my friend's company had a marketing contract with Arnold Palmer, and my friend was scheduled to play a round with him the following week. My friend knew how much we loved Arnie, so he invited me to bring my dad and join the group. We could hardly contain our excitement. Imagine you're the biggest, nerdiest Trekkie in the world, and you've just been invited to have dinner with William Shatner and Leonard Nimoy. You're taken on board the *Starship Enterprise* because dinner just happens to be somewhere over in the next galaxy. Your adrenaline pumps as the great ship jumps into warp speed. Now take that level of excitement to the tenth power, and you might get somewhere close to the "high" we were on. My dad was worried he might not even be able to hold a club in his hands!

Needless to say, we had a blast! Arnie is a great sportsman who gets excited when you make a good shot. And if you hit a really big drive, he'd look at you and make you growl with him like an animal. (It's a guy thing. We dig growling.) So, we'd have a Tim Allen *Tool Time* moment, and we loved it! How is it that one of the greatest golfers of all time, then in his late sixties, could still be that passionate about playing golf with just normal people like me and my dad? There was no crowd watching, but it didn't matter to Arnie. His love of the game was obvious and an inspiration to everyone fortunate enough to be around him. This was why people revered him and joined Arnie's Army, a legion of devoted fans worldwide. He loved what he did, loved playing with people who loved the game, and always gave his best for the fans each and every week—and they felt it.

But that's not the end of the story. The best was yet to come. On the par four 15th hole, our team was tied for the lead. Arnie was four feet away for birdie. My dad was still forty yards from the green with only two shots left to make par. Arnie ran up to my dad and said, "Frank, I need you here. Everyone else is in trouble. All you need to do is chip up on the green and make a two putt. If you can do it you'll get a five on the hole. But with your handicap stroke, it will give us a par. I'll make the birdie and guess what, guys? We'll be in the lead! So put it up there Frank. I need you."

After he finished reviewing the strategy, Arnie walked away toward the green. Dad looked at me and said, "Oh no! He *needs* me! The King of Golf—*needs* me. What do I do?"

I laughed and said, "Well, don't hit your wedge, or you'll chili dip it two inches." I could see the fear written all over his face. He didn't want to let the King down. I told him to take a seven iron and treat it like a putter, using it to putt the ball toward the green. I know he heard me because he nodded his head, but by now he was beginning to hyperventilate. "Don't worry," I said. "Just say, *'One, two,'* and hit it."

He did just as I said . . . One, two, and boink! He hit the ball. It jumped toward the green, bounced up, and picked up speed until—bam! It hit the pin and dropped into the hole! *It actually went in!* My dad chipped in from forty yards out and made birdie on the hole! With his handicap stroke, it was an eagle for the team!

Arnie was now leaping, jumping, and screaming as he ran to my dad and jumped into his arms! He grabbed my dad by the shoulders and shook him and said, "Frank, you really showed me something!" All the way to the green, Arnie had his arm over my dad's shoulder like they were best friends. What a moment! Arnie sank his birdie as well, and once again they high-fived each other like two young kids. My dad's face was aglow! On the next hole, after we all teed off, Dad leaned over and whispered to me, "Bob, I can die a happy man now!" I will never forget how Arnie made that moment special for my dad.

A MOMENT WITH HERB AND MYRNA

An amazing thing also happened to me and my youngest daughter, Rachel. Our family was on a ski vacation in Beaver Creek, Colorado. My two oldest girls were out snowboarding with my wife while Rachel and I were dragging behind, still tired from the previous day. We had just gotten into the back of a long line to take the chair lift up the mountain. That's when we first saw Myrna and Herb, an elderly couple just getting off the bus below. Rachel commented that the man looked to be at least eighty years old. She asked me if I thought he was actually going to ski on such an icy day. I pondered the old guy and finally said, "Maybe so." But inwardly I agreed with Rachel. It looked a little too dangerous for them to be coming up those icy stairs carrying skis and boots. We looked to see if they were with other people who would be helping them. But no, they were on their own. So, the moment presented itself. Do we go about our day and board the lift? Or stop and help this couple?

Rachel and I decided to help. We got out of line and took off our skis, then carefully made our way down the icy stairs. "Hi," I said, "I'm Bob and this is my ten-year-old daughter, Rachel. Are you going to ski today, or just get lunch?"

Myrna said today was Herb's eighty-third birthday, and it was his tradition to come to Colorado and ski a different mountain each year. This year it was Beaver Creek. Herb and I shook hands and he asked if I could grab his skis and boots from the back of the bus. He must have thought I worked there. "Sure," I said. Rachel offered Myrna a hand while I helped Herb up the stairs. His steps were labored, and that concerned me. How was he going to be able to ski down this big mountain?

Myrna and Rachel struck up a conversation and quickly became friends. She complained that this silly tradition of Herb's had to end, but he just grunted and replied, "Nonsense!" Herb didn't have a lift ticket and the ticket office was a good, hearty ten-minute walk from where we were. I asked Herb if he would like for me to handle that for him. He replied enthusiastically, "Great!" After returning with the ticket, I asked if I could help buckle his ski boots. "Please!" he gratefully responded. Buckling boots in the thin air of Colorado can leave you dizzy and light-headed even if you're young and strong. It looked almost impossible for eighty-three-year-old Herb. The next problem was getting Herb to the lift line. At this particular ski resort, you have to cross-country ski for a good ways before you get to the lift. It's very tiring, to say the least. I watched Herb try to push his way to the line, but to no avail. Myrna urged him not to go, but Herb was determined. So Rachel and I pushed him to the front of the lift line. I asked one of the ski patrols to go up the lift with Herb and quietly requested, "Would you please watch Herb?" He couldn't, but assured me there was ski patrol all the way down the mountain. So, off Herb went, cheerfully waving good-bye.

Rachel and I donned our skis and made three trips up and down the mountain having the time of our life. When we finished our third run, we began thinking about Herb, wondering how he was doing. Rachel and I decided to check up on him and found our way back over to Myrna. She was still in the same spot where we had left her reading a book.

"Hi, Myrna, where's Herb?" I asked. She looked concerned, her eyes almost screaming for help. We assured her we would find him and bring him back. That seemed to calm her down somewhat. Amazingly, we found him way over on the right side of the bottom slope just standing there, waiting. "Hey, Herb, it's Bob and Rachel," I said. "How was the run?"

He was covered in snow, obviously from several falls, but he seemed to be in fine shape. He heartily replied, "Couldn't be better, young man!" He glowed with pride at having skied down yet another Colorado mountain—this time at eighty-three!

Rachel congratulated him and told him Myrna was worried. We took off our skis and pushed old Herb a good two hundred yards back to where he had started. By now, I was feeling eighty-three! We took off his boots, found his shoes, and sat with them listening as Herb reviewed the highlights of his ski run. Once again we packed them up and held their arms as they negotiated the icy stairs back down to the minibus. They offered quick thanks, and soon the door closed and the van took off. But after going just about ten yards it came to a stop. Rachel and I looked back and saw Myrna get out of the van. She ran back to me and hugged me—hard. She had tears in her eyes.

"I don't know who you are, young man," she said, "but today, you're my angel. I can't tell you how much you did for me today, and you, too, Rachel. I was so worried coming here. Herb wouldn't listen to me, so I just prayed for help and guidance. I didn't know how we were going to make it. Then all of a sudden—the two of you were there. Herb will never forget your kindness in helping him today."

She didn't know if this was his last run, at eighty-three, but she knew he would surely boast about it to his friends and family all year! The van operator yelled for Myrna and off she went!

What an incredible adventure we all shared that day. It all started with a glance. We noticed some people who seemed to be in a difficult spot, so Rachel and I began asking the questions that would guide us to get involved with total strangers who needed our help. "Are they actually here to ski? How will they get up those steps with these icy conditions? Why isn't there someone to help them? I wonder if we should help?" Questions that required responses that led to making choices. Life is made up of moments and choices. Rachel and I never knew what we were getting ourselves into that icy day in Colorado, but, looking back, we made the best choice of our entire year. A choice we would cherish for years to come.

Dr. Dan Baker, author of the runaway best seller *What Happy People Know,* conducted an exhaustive twenty-five-year study of what actually makes people happy. Surprisingly, it wasn't money, position, fame, or sex. The top two reasons for enduring happiness, it turns out, are *"Gratitude and Giving."* Dr. Baker's study revealed that when people are truly *grateful* for what they have or when they deliberately choose to be *givers,* there is a chemical that gets released in the brain that creates a sense of euphoria, an inner peace, and a feeling of personal significance.

The great motivational speaker Zig Ziglar once said:

{ ! } "You can have everything in life you want if you will just help others get what they want."

Giving is such an essential part of the Power of *"WHO!"* Giving unconditionally releases joy within you that you never knew existed. What would the world be like if everyone helped their *"Who"* World intentionally? Once we change our paradigm from "Me first," "Me alone," and "I can do it by myself," to "How I can help you?" "What do you need?" and "Yes, I will help," then everything in our lives will change for the better.

Wasn't life meant to be simpler than what we've made it? Many of us are working way too hard in jobs we don't like while pursuing relationships that are actually bad for us and in some cases even living in places we don't enjoy. If you allow yourself to be fooled into pursuing just position, power, and money, you will miss out on the true treasures of peace, happiness, and a deep-down contentment. These are the things that truly satisfy. The world will distract you. If you're not careful, you will actually forget *"Who you are"* and end up settling for a second- or third-best identity. Have you put your dreams and goals on hold? Have you settled for a counterfeit destiny? Perhaps it's time to begin to remember . . .

I want to challenge you on two fronts:

1. Remember . . . the times in your life when others were "moment makers" for you. Perhaps it was someone who helped you through a difficult passage in your life or got you that important interview or hired you when no one else would or gave you a great reference— "just because."

2. Step outside your comfort zone, even when it's seemingly inconvenient, to be a "moment maker" for others.

Kevin Spacey starred in a motion picture called *Pay It Forward*, playing a high school teacher who assigned each student in his class to think of a way to make a significant impact in the lives of others. He challenged them to come up with ideas on how their class could change the world for the better. One of the students presented a simple, yet profound idea that required everyone in the class to perform three unconditional acts of kindness for a total stranger with the only stipulation being that the recipient would go and do the same thing for three other people. The concept was to "pay it forward," thereby creating an exponential effect that would change the world for the better.

It's basically the same concept we have seen or experienced at sporting events called the "wave." A group of people stand up and throw their arms in the air then sit back down. The "pay it forward" concept kicks in as the next group of people repeats the process. On and on it goes as the "wave" undulates all around the stadium. You can have the same effect on your world as you look for opportunities to be a giver who creates special moments for others. Just like Arnie or Charlie, you have the power to start a "wave" that just might go around the world. But remember, you don't start a "wave" with the person on the other side of the stadium. You start with the person right next to you!

ABOUT THE AUTHOR

Bob Beaudine is the President & CEO of Eastman & Beaudine, Inc., the trusted and recognized leader in executive search among sports/entertainment/business clients seeking direction, assessment, and counsel in helping shape their leadership teams. In an industry with more than 6,000 competitors, his company was recognized as one of the top fifty recruiting firms in the country. *Sports Illustrated* recently said "Beaudine is the top front office matchmaker in sports" and *The Wall Street Journal* named Eastman & Beaudine the "Top executive recruiting firm in College Sports."

Bob is a high-energy, high-content, engaging speaker with that rare and indefinable ability to inspire others at a deep level. He is sought out by many of the nation's business, sports, and entertainment organizations to speak at conferences, conventions, and workshops. Bob consults industry executives who are seeking their unique path in life. He has interviewed and coached senators, governors, generals, CEO's, university presidents, top athletic directors, coaches, and Hollywood studio executives.

Bob's leadership extends into his local community where he served as Chairman of the "Doak Walker National Running Back Award." He is a member of SMU Cox School of Business Associate Board. He is a graduate (1977) of Southern Methodist University with a bachelor of business administration degree. He and his wife Cheryl have been married for twenty-five years and have three fabulous daughters, ages twenty-three, twenty-two, and eighteen, and reside in Plano, Texas.